Rediscovering the Meaning of Christmas

GOD WITH US

Scott Cairns

Emilie Griffin

Richard John Neuhaus

Kathleen Norris

Eugene Peterson

Luci Shaw

Edited by Greg Pennoyer and Gregory Wolfe

PARACLETE PRESS
BREWSTER, MASSACHUSETTS

God with Us: Rediscovering the Meaning of Christmas

2008   Second Printing
2007   First Printing

Copyright © 2007 by Greg Pennoyer

ISBN: 978-1-55725-541-9

Library of Congress Cataloging-in-Publication Data
God with us : rediscovering the meaning of Christmas / Scott Cairns ... [et al] ;
edited by Greg Pennoyer and Gregory Wolfe.
    p. cm. ISBN 978-1-55725-541-9
 1. Advent—Meditations. 2. Christmas—Meditations. 3. Epiphany—Meditations. I. Cairns, Scott. II. Pennoyer, Greg. III. Wolfe, Gregory.
BV40.G58 2007
242'.33—dc22   2007021985

10 9 8 7 6 5 4 3 2

Published by Paraclete Press
Brewster, Massachusetts
www.paracletepress.com

Printed in Malaysia

contents

Contents

Histories of the Feast Days
Beth Bevis

preface

Greg Pennoyer

THIS BOOK IS THE RESULT OF A JOURNEY that began on Christmas morning, 1998, in Ottawa in a small Anglo-Catholic church called St. Barnabas. It was my first encounter with what my high church friends call "smells and bells." Throughout that Christmas service a translucent ribbon of incense lingered just above eye level. Its constant presence provided a gentle introduction to the physical elements of the Christmas service that I had not experienced before—the Eucharist, the processions, the sights, sounds, and, yes, smells.

It was a mystery to me at the time, but I left the church that Christmas morn with a sense that I had worshipped God with all my senses—with my whole being—for the first time in my life.

My journey into the heart of the church's liturgical and spiritual theology continues, but in a strange way it keeps returning me, again and again, to Christmas day. For it is in this great feast—in the celebration of the Incarnation, the Word made flesh—that I can begin to see what an embodied faith might mean.

Like most adults, I have a difficult time relating to Christmas. Having lost the wonder of childhood I try to make up for it through our peculiarly modern mixture of materialism and sentimentality. For me, as for so many people (including millions of believers), Christmas has become a parody of itself.

The more I reflected on my experience at St. Barnabas, the more I realized that my own temptation to sentimentalize Christmas involved turning away from the messiness of my disenchanted, adult life. Christmas is, after all, the story of the Creator entering into his creation—a creation that has been marred by human sin and weakness.

Preface

It is the story of a God who does not disdain this world, despite its frailty, ambiguities, and messiness. The God who became a helpless babe in a stable entered into our human anxieties and confusions and redeemed them.

Christmas is the feast of the Incarnation, which is the mystery of God with us in the flesh. When we cut through the sentiment and marketing to the spiritual riches of Christmas, we recover not only a sense of who God is, but also who *we* are as human beings.

Such a recovery cannot happen in a day. One of the things I have learned about the ancient church is that it knew that real, lasting change comes about over time, which is why it set aside whole seasons for meditation and celebration of the great mysteries of faith. And so the early Christians set Christmas in the larger context of the Advent season that precedes it and the Epiphany season that extends its meaning outward from Bethlehem to the whole world. To live through these seasons is to embark on a pilgrimage through time.

God With Us is intended as a companion and guide for those who would make this journey. Each of the elements of this book—daily meditations, Scripture selections, prayers, histories of the major feast days, along with the classic and contemporary artworks that illustrate these pages—can help us along the path. Together, they weave together the rich tapestry of Christmas, calling us to an embodied faith, one that finds redemption in the messiness of our lives and encounters the divine in the ordinary stuff of this world.

God with us. This is the meaning of the Incarnation. This is the meaning of Christmas.

—GREG PENNOYER

vi

*Greg
Pennoyer*

introduction
Eugene Peterson

Birth: WONDER . . . ASTONISHMENT . . . ADORATION. There can't be very many of us for whom the sheer fact of existence hasn't rocked us back on our heels. We take off our sandals before the burning bush. We catch our breath at the sight of a plummeting hawk. "Thank you, God." We find ourselves in a lavish existence in which we feel a deep sense of kinship—we *belong* here; we say thanks with our lives to Life. And not just "Thanks" or "Thank It" but "Thank *You*." Most of the people who have lived on this planet earth have identified this You with God or gods. This is not just a matter of learning our manners, the way children are taught to say thank you as a social grace. It is the cultivation of adequateness within ourselves to the nature of reality, developing the capacity to sustain an adequate response to the overwhelming gift and goodness of life.

Wonder is the only adequate launching pad for exploring this fullness, this wholeness, of human life. Once a year, each Christmas, for a few days at least, we and millions of our neighbors turn aside from our preoccupations with life reduced to biology or economics or psychology and join together in a community of wonder. The wonder keeps us open-eyed, expectant, alive to life that is always more than we can account for, that always exceeds our calculations, that is always beyond anything we can make.

If in the general festive round of singing and decorating, giving and receiving, cooking meals and family gatherings, we ask what is behind all this and what keeps it going all over the world, among all classes of people quite regardless of whether they believe or not, the answer is simply "a birth." Not just "birth" in general, but a particular birth in a small Middle Eastern village in datable time—a named baby, Jesus—a birth that soon had people talking and singing about God, indeed, *worshiping* God.

This invites reflection. For birth, simply as birth, even though often enough greeted with wonder and accompanied with ceremony and celebration, has a way of getting absorbed into business as usual far too soon. The initial impulses of gratitude turn out to be astonishingly ephemeral. Birth in itself does not seem to compel belief in God. There are plenty of people who take each new life on its own terms and deal with the person just as he or she comes to us, no questions asked. There is something very attractive about this: it is so clean and uncomplicated and noncontroversial. And obvious. They get a satisfying sense of the inherently divine in life itself without all the complications of church: the theology, the mess of church history, the hypocrisies of church-goers, the incompetence of pastors, the appeals for money. Life, as life, seems perfectly capable of furnishing them with a spirituality that exults in beautiful beaches and fine sunsets, surfing and skiing and body massage, emotional states and aesthetic titillation without investing too much God-attentiveness in a baby.

But for all its considerable attractions, this shift of attention from birth to aspects of the world that please us on our terms is considerably deficient in person. Birth means that a *person* is alive in the world. A miracle of sorts, to be sure, but a miracle that very soon gets obscured by late-night feedings, diapers, fevers, and inconvenient irruptions of fussiness and squalling. Soon the realization sets in that we are in for years and years of the child's growing-up time that will stretch our stamina and patience, sometimes to the breaking point.

So how did it happen that *this* birth, this *Jesus* birth managed to set so many of us back on our heels in astonishment and gratitude and wonder? And continues to do so century after century, at least at this time of year?

The brief answer is that this wasn't just any birth. The baby's parents and first witnesses were convinced that God was entering human history in human form. Their conviction was confirmed in angel and Magi and shepherds visitations; eventually an extraordinary life came into being before their eyes, right in their neighborhood. More and more people became convinced. Men, women, and children from all over the world continue to be convinced right up to the present moment.

Birth, every human birth, is an occasion for local wonder. In Jesus' birth the wonder is extrapolated across the screen of all creation and all history as a God-birth. "The Word became flesh and dwelt among us"—moved into the neighborhood, so to speak. And for thirty years or so, men and women saw God in speech and action in the entirely human person of Jesus as he was subject, along with them, to the common historical conditions of, as Charles Williams once put it, "Jewish religion, Roman order, and Greek intellect." These were not credulous people and it was not easy for them to believe, but they did. That God was made incarnate as a human baby is still not easy to believe, but people continue to do so. Many, even those who don't "believe," find themselves happy to participate in the giving and receiving, singing and celebrating of those who do.

Incarnation, *in-flesh-ment,* God in human form in Jesus entering our history: this is what started Christmas. This is what keeps Christmas going.

Christmas, and the Incarnation that it celebrates, has its foundation in creation. The Genesis stories of creation begin with "heaven and earth," but that turns out to be merely a warm-up exercise for the main event, the creation of human life, man and woman designated as the "image of God." Man and woman are alive with the very breath ("spirit") of God. If we want to look at creation full, creation at its highest, we look at a person—a man, a woman, a child. There are those who prefer to gaze on the beauty of a bouquet of flowers rather than care for a squabbling baby, or to spend a day on the beach rather than rub shoulders with uncongenial neighbors in a cold church—creation without the inconvenience of persons. This may be understandable, but it is also decidedly not creation in the terms that have been revealed to us in Genesis and in the person of Jesus.

All this arrives as most welcome good news in the birth of Jesus: here we have creation as God's gift of life, creation furnishing all the conditions necessary for life—*our* lives. Good news, truly, what the Greeks named a *kerygma,* a public proclamation that becomes a historical event. The birth of Jesus is the kerygmatic focus for receiving, entering into, and participating in creation, for *living* the creation and not just using it or taking it for granted.

In the first chapter of St. John's Gospel, his re-writing of Genesis, we read, "the Word became flesh and dwelt among us." St. Matthew and St. Luke begin their Gospel stories with detailed accounts of Jesus' birth. St. Paul in his letter to the Colossians, the first written reference to Jesus' birth, calls Jesus the "first-born of all creation."

Creation is God's work, not ours. We accept and enter into and submit to what God does—what God made and makes. We are not spectators of creation but participants in it. We are participants first of all by simply being born, but then we realize that our births all take place in the defining context of Jesus' birth. The Christian life is the practice of living in what God has done and is doing. We want to know the origins of things so that we can live out of our origins. We don't want our lives to be tacked on to something peripheral. We want to live *origin*-ally, not derivatively.

So we begin with Jesus. Jesus is the revelation of the God who created heaven and earth; he is also the revelation of the God who is with us, Immanuel. The original Genesis creation, the stories of Israel, the lamentations of the prophets, the singing of the psalms—all of these make sense in light of that one birth that we celebrate at Christmas. The theologian Karl Barth goes into immense detail (he wrote four fat volumes on it) to make this single point: "We have established that from every angle Jesus Christ is the key to the secret of creation."

The conception and birth of Jesus is the surprise of creation. "This is God's initiative going beyond anything man or woman has dreamed of." This is the birth that will now set all births under the conditions of God's creative initiative.

By stating that Jesus is "born of woman"—this Mary (as both St. Matthew and St. Luke attest)—St. Paul insists that Jesus is most emphatically human, the "firstborn of all *creation*." That this Mary is at the same time a virgin prevents the birth of Jesus from being reduced to what we know or can reproduce from our own experience. Life that is unmistakably *human* life is before us here, a real baby from an actual mother's womb; there is also miracle here, and mystery that cannot be brushed aside in our attempts to bring the operations of God, let alone our own lives, under our control. The miracle of the virgin birth, maintained from the earliest times in the church and confessed in its creeds, is, in Karl Barth's straightforward phrase, a "summons to *reverence* and *worship*. . . ." Barth maintained that the one-sided views of those who questioned or denied that Jesus was "born of the virgin Mary" are "in the last resort to be understood only as coming from dread of reverence and only as invitation to comfortable encounter with an all too near or all too far-off God."

Artists, poets, musicians, and architects are our primary witnesses to the significance of the meaning of *virgin* in the virgin birth as "a summons to reverence and worship." Over and over again they rescue us from a life in which the wonder has leaked out. While theologians and biblical scholars have argued, sometimes most contentiously, over texts, sexual facts, and mythological parallels, our artists have painted Madonnas, our poets have provided our imaginations with rhythms and metaphors, our musicians have filled the air with carols and anthems that bring us to our knees in adoration, and our architects have designed and built chapels and cathedrals in which we can worship God.

Madeleine L'Engle's poem "After Annunciation" tells us why:

> This is the irrational season
> When love blooms bright and wild.
> Had Mary been filled with reason
> There'd have been no room for the child.

Conception, pregnancy, and birth language that features God as the Creator occupy a prominent place in our Scriptures as they give witness to the Christian life. Jesus' words to Nicodemus about being "born anew" are certainly the most well known. Jesus and Nicodemus between them use the word *born* seven times in the course of their conversation. In an extravagant metaphor Paul sees the entire creation groaning "as if in the pangs of childbirth" in his letter to the Romans. Another time he identified himself to the Galatians as a mother in the pains of childbirth.

The story of Jesus' birth is our entry into understanding and participating in our place in creation. But every birth can, if we let it, return us to the wonder of Jesus' birth, the revelation of sheer life as gift, God's life with us and for us.

God is the Creator, and his most encompassing creation is human life, a baby. We, as participants in creation, do it too. When we beget and conceive, give birth to and raise babies, we are in on the heart of creation. There is more gospel in all those "begats" in the genealogical lists of our Scriptures ("And Ezekias begat Manasses; and Manasses begat Amon; and Amon begat Josias . . .") than we ever dreamed.

Birth, any birth, is our primary access to the creative work of God. And we birth much more than human babies. Our lives give birth to God's kingdom every day—or, at least, they should. And Jesus' virgin birth provides and maintains the focus that God himself is personally present and totally participant in creation; this is good news, indeed. Every birth is kerygmatic. The birth of Jesus, kept fresh in our imaginations and prayers in song and story, keeps our feet on solid ground and responsive to every nuance of obedience and praise evoked by the life all around us.

But the actual birth of Jesus has never been an easy truth for people to swallow. There are always plenty of people around who will have none of this particularity: human ordinariness, body fluid, raw emotions of anger and disgust, fatigue and loneliness. Birth is painful. Babies are inconvenient and messy. There is immense trouble in having children. God having a baby? It's far easier to accept God as the creator of the majestic mountains, the rolling sea, and the delicate wild flowers.

When it comes to the sordid squalor of the raw material involved in being human, God is surely going to keep his distance. Or, is he? We may fantasize deep aspirations native to our souls that abhor this business of diapers and debts, government taxes and domestic trivia. Deep in our bones we may have the sense that we must have been created for higher things, that there is a world of subtle ideas and fine feelings and exquisite ecstasies for us to cultivate.

Somewhere along the way some of us become convinced that *our* souls are *different*—a cut above the masses, the common herd of philistines that trample the courts of the Lord. Such people become connoisseurs of the sublime.

As it turned out, the ink was barely dry on the stories telling of the birth of Jesus before people were busy putting out alternate stories that were more "spiritual" than those provided in our Gospels. A rash of apocryphal stories, with Jesus smoothed out and universalized, flooded the early church. They were immensely popular. They still are. And people are still writing them. These alternate stories prove very attractive to a lot of people.

In these accounts of the Christian life, the hard-edged particularities of Jesus' life are blurred into the sublime divine. The hard, historical factuality of the Incarnation, the Word made flesh as God's full and complete revelation of himself, is dismissed as crude. Something finer and more palatable to sensitive souls is put in its place: "Jesus was not truly flesh and blood, but entered a human body temporarily in order to give us the inside story on God and initiate us into the secrets of the spiritual life." And, "Of course he didn't die on the cross, but made his exit at the last minute. The body that was taken from the cross for burial was not Jesus at all, but a kind of costume he used for a few years and then discarded."

It turns out in these versions that Jesus merely role-played a historical flesh-and-blood Christ for a brief time and then returned to a purely spiritual realm. If we accept that version of Jesus, we are then free to live the version: we put up with materiality and locale and family for as much and as long as necessary, but only for as much and as long as necessary. The material, the physical, the body—history and geography and weather, *people*—are temporary scaffolding; the sooner we realize that none of it has anything to do with God and Jesus, the better.

The attractions of employing this temporary scaffolding are considerable. For those of us who take this point of view, the feature attraction is that we no longer have to take seriously either things or people. Anything we can touch, smell, or see is not of God in any direct or immediate way. We save ourselves an enormous amount of inconvenience and aggravation by putting materiality and everydayness at the edge of our lives, at least our spiritual lives. Mountains are nice as long as they inspire lofty thoughts, but if one stands in the way of our convenience, a bulldozer can be called in to get rid of it. Other people are glorious as long as they are good-looking and well-mannered, bolster our self-esteem, and help us fulfill our human potential, but if they somehow bother us they certainly deserve to be dismissed.

But it's hard to maintain this view of things through the Christmas season. There is too much stuff, too many *things*. And all of it festively connects up with Jesus and God. Every year Christmas comes around again and forces us to deal with God in the context of demanding and inconvenient children; gatherings of family members, many of whom we spend the rest of the year avoiding; all the crasser forms of greed and commercialized materiality; garish lights and decorations. Or maybe the other way around: Christmas forces us to deal with all the mess of our humanity in the context of God who has already entered that mess in the glorious birth of Jesus.

Cohen, *The Creation of the World*

living the church year:
an invitation

W HAT DOES IT MEAN TO "LIVE THE CHURCH YEAR"? Our goal is to recover a more ancient way of looking at time and the mysterious relationship between the material and spiritual realms.

The early Christians believed that the rhythm of the year gave us a perfect opportunity to re-enact the story of our salvation. In the holy days and seasons of the church year, the life of Christ and the entirety of human history are recapitulated. The eternal is aligned with the here and now.

God With Us is an introduction to the first three "seasons" of the Church calendar. Advent begins this sacred year because it looks forward to Christ's birth, the event that brings about the "new creation" of a people redeemed by God. Christmas celebrates Christ's Incarnation and Epiphany his "manifestation" to the whole world.

Later, in Lent, we have another time of preparation as we look to the Passion on Good Friday and the Resurrection on Easter Sunday. After the Easter season comes Pentecost, which recounts the descent of the Holy Spirit on the disciples and the beginning of the church's life on earth. Finally, the long season of "ordinary time" after Pentecost reminds us of the story we are living now: the church in time. At the end of ordinary time we look to the end of time . . . and then with Advent we begin the cycle again.

Another layer of the Church year involves remembering those in human history who have lived extraordinarily holy lives, and who thus serve as models for us. So the seasons are punctuated by memorial days that celebrate the saints and martyrs of the church.

The act of remembering becomes effective in our lives only when we share that memory with others. We do that through worship, and in particular through the corporate act of worship known as liturgy. The Greek word for liturgy means "the work of the people." It is constituted by the actions we take—the physical gestures, prayers, or other customs—that make faith a tangible presence in our lives.

Liturgy, too, is incarnational, involving our bodily and sensory participation in worship. Each season in the liturgical year, then, comes with its own set of traditions—sights, smells, and sounds that involve our senses; and readings, prayers, and practices that call us to undertake certain activities. Each of the seasons and holy days of the church year is marked by practices that reflect the meaning of that season or day. There are times for feasting and for fasting, preparation and celebration.

The brief histories of the major feast days that follow include information about the traditions, both liturgical and popular, that have become associated with the seasons of Advent, Christmas, and Epiphany. The meaning of the Incarnation unfolds for us in the myriad gestures of prayer and worship that help us to align our lives with the rhythm of the church year.

GOD WITH US

Gauguin, *Nativity.*

history of the feast

WHEN SOMEONE WE LOVE COMES TO VISIT—when a child returns home for a holiday or an old friend from far away finally comes to town—we are full of anticipation and prepare to receive our guest with joy. We may even clean the house and polish the silver.

So it is with Advent, the season set aside by the ancient Christian communities to prepare for the mystery we are about to celebrate at Christmas: the arrival of God with us, God incarnate.

The season of Advent begins on the fourth Sunday before Christmas. While our contemporary consumer culture begins the process of celebrating Christmas right after Thanksgiving—with relentless marketing and an endless soundtrack of carols and songs—liturgical tradition takes a different approach. In liturgical churches you won't hear carols or see a Christmas tree in the sanctuary during Advent— those festivities are reserved for Christmas. Advent, by contrast, is a more solemn season of preparation and anticipation. We set aside these four weeks to prepare ourselves to receive this great mystery into our hearts.

In some churches, beginning on the first Sunday of Advent, several changes become evident. According to tradition, the usual "Gloria in Excelsis" in the Sunday liturgy is omitted. Clergy wear robes of purple— the same color worn during Lent—to remind us of the solemn nature of the season.

These changes alert us to the fact that Advent is also a time to practice certain spiritual disciplines. Just as we might clean our house in preparation for the arrival of a special guest, so church tradition asks us to take stock of our souls and be at our best when the special day arrives.

Christians through the ages have looked upon this combination of celebration and solemnity not as a contradiction, but as a meaningful paradox. The practice of self-discipline during Advent helps us to make more room for joy so that we are fully prepared to receive the Lord when he comes.

The Advent wreath is perhaps the most beloved of many Advent traditions, both in the home and in the church. Wreaths are fashioned out of evergreens and decorated with four candles, one for each Sunday leading up to Christmas. Sometimes a fifth candle, representing Christ, is placed in the center of the wreath and is lit at Christmas. Advent wreaths function as a focus for family prayer during these weeks: parents say prayers of preparation for Christ's arrival, and children often help to light candles in the wreath. Each Sunday candles are lit in order to mark the progression of time and increase our sense of anticipation as we approach the day of Christ's birth. The candle flame is a reminder of the light that comes into the world at Christmas.

Throughout Advent, Christians prepare their hearts not only for the celebration of Christmas, but also for the many ways that Christ breaks into the world—past, present, and future. We prepare for the celebration of the anniversary of God's first coming into the world; we prepare for the many ways in which he comes to us now; and we look forward to his future coming in glory at the end of time.

Richard John Neuhaus
First Sunday of Advent

Scripture: *Isaiah 2:1–5; Psalm 121;*
Romans 13:11–14; Matthew 24:37–44

W E ARE ALL SEARCHING, AND ULTIMATELY—whether we know it or not—we are searching for God. Ultimately, we are searching for the Ultimate, and the Ultimate is God. It is not easy, searching for God, but maybe your reading this book is part of your own searching. The fact is that we do not really *know* what we're looking for or who we're looking for. Almost a thousand years ago, St. Anselm of Canterbury said, "God is that greater than which cannot be thought."

Think about it. We can stretch our minds as high and deep and far as our minds can stretch, and at the point of the highest, deepest, farthest stretch of our minds, we have not "thought" God. There is always a thought beyond what we are able to think. "God is that greater than which cannot be thought."

God is, quite literally, inconceivable. And that is why God was conceived as a human being in the womb of the Virgin Mary. Because we cannot, even in thought, rise up to God, God stooped down to us in Jesus, who is "Emmanuel," which means "God with us."

As we are searching for God, the good news is that God is searching for us. Better yet, he has found us. The great question is not whether we have found God but whether we have found ourselves being found by God. God is not lost. *We* were, or, as the case may be, we *are*. There are many ways of being lost. Listen to the words of Jesus in Matthew 24. As in the days of Noah before that great flood, we were lost in eating and drinking, in marrying and giving in marriage. In a word, we were lost in living what we told ourselves was the good life. We wanted more and more of it, and the more we had of it the more we longed for what

Bosch, *Adoration of the Magi.*

Bosch, *Adoration of the Magi.*

was beyond the reach of our longing or the grasp of our possessing. In our longing and our searching, we were blind to the gift already given, Emmanuel: God with us.

Here is what St. Paul says: "It is full time now for you to wake from sleep." He is telling us to wake up to the gift already given. This season of the Church's calendar is called Advent, which means "coming." Christ came, Christ comes, Christ will come again. There is no time— past, present, or future—in which Jesus the Christ (which means Jesus the anointed one) is not God with us. He was with you yesterday, is with you today, and will be with you tomorrow. So we are invited to give up our searching and let ourselves be found by the One who wants to be with us, and to have us with him, forever.

We are forever seeking, while the forever for which we seek is now. Awaken to the truth that any place contains every place and every moment contains eternity. And that is because Christ is Emmanuel, the One whom the Book of Revelation calls the Alpha and Omega, the beginning and the end. (Alpha and Omega are the first and last letters of the Greek alphabet. We might say that he is the A and the Z.) He is the Word of God who called into being everything that is or ever has been or ever will be. He is the One in whom past, present, and future are always now.

Seekers and searchers of all times have looked toward the heavens in order to find God. Then the gift was given. Mary's searching was interrupted by an angel who promised that soon, very soon, in a matter of nine months, she would look not up but down, into the face of the baby in her arms, into the face of God. This is called *incarnation*, meaning that God is enfleshed in our humanity.

She said to the angel, "Let it be to me according to your word." And so it was. And so it is with all who, wearied by their searching, wake up to the gift already given; so it is with all who wake up to find themselves found by Emmanuel, God with us.

prayer

20

Richard John Neuhaus

Father in heaven, you came to earth in the person of your Son, Jesus Christ. As the coming of your Spirit upon Mary inspired her to welcome the One who is her child and her lord, so also open our eyes to the gift already given. Forgive us our restless searching for your presence according to our expectations. Direct our searching according to your gift. May we, like the star-led sages of old, be ever guided to the appointed meeting place in the Child of Bethlehem.

In him and by him, let us be found by you. With your apostle Paul we would put on the Lord Jesus Christ, wearing his humility as our robe of splendor. Forbid that we seek any glory that is not his. In his childhood, we become as little children. In his teaching, we are trained to delight you by our service. In his miracles, we are changed, like water into wine, our vain ambitions transformed into obedience to your call. In his suffering and death, we share in his victory over every wrong within us and without.

Fill, we pray you, our every moment with his threefold advent. As then he came and now he comes and will one day come again, awaken us to the then and now and one day of his presence in this present moment. As we put on the Lord Jesus Christ, may all our time be clothed by eternity until we find ourselves at last in the home you have prepared for seekers and searchers who, in our seeking and searching, were hopelessly lost. Give us, we pray, the grace to surrender to being found.

This we ask in the name above every name, the name of Jesus Christ. Amen. Let it be.

first monday of Advent

Scripture: *Isaiah 2:1–5; Matthew 8:5–11, 13*

Richard John Neuhaus

MATTHEW'S GOSPEL TELLS US about the centurion at Capernaum who asks Jesus to heal his servant in distress. "I will come and heal him," says Jesus. To which the centurion responds, "Lord, I am not worthy to have you come under my roof; but only say the word, and my servant will be healed." Jesus says the word and the servant is healed. Of the Roman centurion he then says, "Not even in Israel have I found such faith."

Faith does not assert claims; faith receives the gift that is undeserved. Faith is itself a gift, the gift of receptivity. Mary received the gift in saying, "Let it be to me according to your word." To her, and through her to us, was given the gift of the Child who is nothing less, no one less, than the Savior of the world. For us he lived and suffered and died; for us he was raised triumphant that we might, even though we suffer and die, forever live in his glory. The gift is already given and forever is now for those who give him permission to let life be a gift in response to gift. It really is a matter of giving God permission, as Mary gave God permission. He will not be the Lord of our life without our permission. Faith is giving permission.

"Lord, I am not worthy." On our lips and in our hearts, these are words of surrendering love—of love surrendering to love. They are words by which we empty ourselves, by which we open ourselves, to receive the gift. If we are full of ourselves, complaining about what we deserve and do not deserve, there is no room in our hearts to receive the gift. If we deserved the gift, it would not be a gift. "Lord, I am not worthy." With these words, we make room in our hearts for the gift.

Veronese, *The Centurion of Capernaum.*

Veronese, *The Centurion of Capernaum*.

Christmas is the giving and receiving of gifts. What a joy. What a hassle. What gifts to give to whom? What gifts to expect in return? The hassle surrenders to gratitude as we, setting aside all calculations of who deserves what, respond by giving as we have been given. "Lord, I am not worthy." With these words, complaints and grievances are banished. With these words, the gift is given to receive the gift of giving. With these words, faith gives permission for Christ to be in our lives Emmanuel, God with us.

23

Richard John Neuhaus

Lord Jesus Christ, like the centurion's servant, we are in distress. Save us from the sin of presumption and complaint, for we have no claim on your love other than the promise that you love us. Purge us, cleanse us, empty us, open us, so that our every moment becomes a gift in response to your gift of life eternal, beginning now. Amen. Let it be.

prayer

de Nomé, *Fantastic Ruins with Saint Augustine and the Child.*

First Tuesday of Advent

Scripture: *Isaiah 11:1–10; Luke 10:21–24*

WILL IT REALLY HAPPEN? Will it really happen that one day the wolf will lie down with the lamb, and the leopard with the baby goat, and the lion with the calf, and "a little child shall lead them"? Such, says the prophet Isaiah, is the promise of the Peaceable Kingdom. In our unpeaceable world, we long for the fulfillment of the promise. In a time of war—remembering that every moment of history is a time of war—I watch a young woman standing vigil at the corner of Fifth Avenue and 20th Street holding her poignant placard, "Peace is Possible." She is right, although maybe not in the way she intends.

Born into a world of raging conflicts, the little child who leads us is called the Prince of Peace. Above the fields of Bethlehem, the angels sang at his birth, "Glory to God in the highest, and on earth peace among men with whom he is pleased." Yet what a strange Prince of Peace is this. "Woe to those," he said, "who cry peace, peace when there is no peace." He also said: "Peace I leave with you; my peace I give to you; not as the world gives do I give to you. Let not your hearts be troubled, neither let them be afraid." Peace is not only possible; it is the gift already given. Christ gives us his peace by giving us himself, for he is the Prince of Peace.

For peace in the world we must fervently pray and earnestly work. But do not be troubled or frightened by the wars around you and the wars within you. We are keenly aware of the warfare. The peace that is ours is not a peace of pretending that things are not as they are; nor is it a peace of being blind to conflict. It is the peace of faith.

Geoffroy, *The Resigned.*

26

Richard John Neuhaus

Faith is trust in the Prince of Peace. We neither hold ourselves aloof from the anguish of a conflicted world nor delude ourselves that the resolution of all conflicts is within our power. In the child of Bethlehem, in the powerlessness of a baby, God entered into our conflicts. The powers of darkness and death raged against his intrusion and did their worst, beginning with murderous King Herod, who killed the babies of Bethlehem, and ending with a cruel death on a cross.

The dark and deadly powers still rage because they know they have been defeated by the Prince of Peace—incarnate, crucified, and crowned in glory. By faith in him and the victory that he won, we already live in the Peaceable Kingdom that is to be. Because it *has* really happened, it *will* really happen. And Jesus said, "Fear not, little flock, for it is your Father's good pleasure to give you the kingdom." Fear not.

prayer

Heavenly Father, look out for your children who are imperiled by war around us and war within us. Prepare us to welcome the Prince of Peace in his birth at Bethlehem so that in a violent world he may make us instruments of the peace that he gives. Amen. Let it be.

Scripture: *Isaiah 25:6–10a;*
Matthew 15:29–37

27

Richard John
Neuhaus

D ID THAT REALLY HAPPEN? In Matthew 15 we read that Jesus took seven loaves of bread and a few fish, he gave thanks and broke them, and with them he fed a hungry crowd of about eight thousand people (assuming there were as many women and children as there were men). Similar events are related in the other Gospel accounts. Incredible? Many people think so. Even some Christians are embarrassed by these miracle reports and try to ignore them or explain them away. After all, we simply *know* that you can't feed thousands of people with seven loaves and a few fish.

With this we are brought to the central mystery of Christmas—not a mystery that is like a puzzle to be solved, but a mystery that is a deep truth to be endlessly explored. "With God all things are possible," Jesus said. And the deepest of deep truths about Christmas—without which Christmas is just a lovely social custom—is that Mary's baby is God. He is God incarnate, which means God become one of us, which means he is true God and true man. The challenge to faith is not that he fed so many with so little, or that he healed the sick, or that he gave sight to the blind, or any of the other astonishing things reported. The challenge to faith is that he is "Emmanuel, God with us." If that is true, with him all things are possible.

There is a wonder-full Latin phrase in Christian theology: *Finitum capax infiniti*—the finite is capable of the infinite. We who are created by God are created finite. Our lives are bounded by space and time; at any one time we can be in only one place or another, and there is a date on the calendar for our birth, and for our death. We are mortal. We are finite. In the child of Mary, our three-dimensional, time-bounded

Giovane, *Miracle of the Loaves and Fishes.*

existence is penetrated by the eternal infinite. *Finitum capax infiniti* means that now, because of Emmanuel, the creation is riddled through and through, is electrically charged with, the presence of God. This baby is in human form the Word of God by whom and for whom all things came to be.

John chapter one: "In the beginning was the Word, and the Word was with God, and the Word was God. . . . All things were made through him, and without him was not anything made that was made. In him was life, and the life was the light of men. The light shines in the darkness, and the darkness has not overcome it." The darkness will not overcome it. Never, never ever.

Giving sight to the blind, turning water into wine, feeding thousands with a few loaves and fish—these and other miracles are aimed at alerting us to the miracle of Emmanuel, God with us. If we believe that *that* is what happened at Christmas, all difficulties about other miracles in the Gospel accounts are resolved. The Gospel accounts call the miracles of Jesus "signs." The miracles are signs pointing beyond themselves to Jesus Christ, true God and true man, in whom is revealed the stupendous fact that *finitum capax infiniti.*

28

Richard John Neuhaus

prayer

Awaken, O Lord Jesus, our hearts and minds to your presence in the world of your love's creating. Forbid that we should stumble through this day oblivious to the wonder in the ordinary. With your grace, startle us into faith's perception of your continuing creation in our lives. Amen. Let it be.

Giovane, *Miracle of the Loaves and Fishes*.

First Thursday of Advent

Scripture: *Isaiah 26:1–6;*
Matthew 6:25–33; 7:21, 24–27

Richard John
Neuhaus

THEREFORE I TELL YOU, DO NOT BE ANXIOUS ABOUT YOUR LIFE." That is what Jesus says, but is it really possible to live without anxieties both big and small? We are anxious about children, friends, jobs, health—and the list goes on and on. We are anxious about so many things.

There is unbelieving anxiety, and then there is anxiety encountered by faith. John Henry Newman said of Christian faith, "Ten thousand difficulties do not add up to a doubt." We may have great difficulties in understanding *how* God will keep his promises, but we do not doubt *that* he will keep his promises.

Mary was anxious when the angel appeared out of nowhere announcing, "Hail, O favored one, the Lord is with you." Luke tells us, "But she was greatly troubled at the saying, and considered in her mind what sort of greeting this might be." Mary had good reason to be troubled. She might well have thought, *What are people going to say and do about a young girl who is pregnant, and not by her husband?* Mary did not know what was going to happen next. She did not have at hand a catechism or a theology textbook to look up the meaning of "incarnation." Mary was anxious.

To be anxious is to be human. The question is what we do with our anxieties. The decision is between hanging on to them or handing them over. After listening to the angel, Mary handed over herself, including her anxieties. "Behold, I am the handmaid of the Lord; let it be to me according to your word." That is Mary's great *fiat*—"Let it be." It is not fatalism, but faith. Fatalism is resigning ourselves to the inevitable; faith is entrusting ourselves to the One who is eternally trustworthy, who is worthy of trust.

Poussin, *The Annunciation.*

32

Richard John Neuhaus

"Let it be to me according to your word." At the very beginning of the Christian story, the theme is set for the people beyond numbering who will come to recognize the child of Mary as their Lord. He most perfectly handed himself over to his Father, who is also our Father. In the Garden of Gethsemane, the night before he died, he prayed: "Not my will but yours be done." He is not *resigned* to the Father's will; he *embraces* the Father's will. Accepting God's way is not a fallback position for when we can't get our way.

"Let it be to me according to your word." Faith is not blind faith, but trust with eyes wide open. Faith does not deny the reason for anxiety but rejects the rule of anxiety. Ten thousand difficulties do not add up to a doubt. In the "Our Father," Jesus teaches us to pray, "your will be done, on earth as it is in heaven." Slowly, and not without difficulty, we learn to prefer God's will to our own; we learn to *want* God's will to be done, knowing that he knows us and loves us immeasurably better than we know and love ourselves.

"Therefore I tell you, do not be anxious about your life." Mary was greatly troubled. She surrendered herself, and with herself she surrendered her troubles, with eyes wide open. She handed over her anxieties, and thus did she receive the gift of faith, and thus do we receive the gift of faith today, the gift of Emmanuel, God with us.

prayer

Forgive us, Heavenly Father, for living as though you do not know and do not care, as though you are not our loving Father. As you did with Mary, who first received the good news of "Emmanuel, God with us," and handed over her troubled heart to you, so also give us such faith that the constant theme of our lives may be, "Lord, let it be to me according to your word." This we trustingly ask in the name of Jesus Christ, her Lord and ours. Amen. Let it be.

First Friday of Advent

Scripture: *Isaiah 29:17–24; Matthew 9:27–31*

Richard John Neuhaus

I T IS JUST AS THE PROPHET ISAIAH SAID 700 YEARS before the birth of Jesus: the deaf shall hear and the blind shall see. It will happen "in that day," said Isaiah. The angels over the fields of Bethlehem announced the coming of that day. That day will continue until the end of time. That day is now.

The two blind men were persistent. Like so many who came to Jesus in their neediness, they were not afraid of making a nuisance of themselves. Their persistence was matched by their faith. Jesus asks, "Do you believe that I am able to do this?" They answer with a simple, "Yes, Lord." We read, "Then he touched their eyes, saying, 'According to your faith be it done to you.' And their eyes were opened." In the new day predicted by Isaiah and inaugurated by the birth of Jesus, we bring to Christ our need and receive according to our faith, knowing that our faith is his greatest gift.

Miracles happened, and miracles happen now. The world is wilder and more wondrous than most of us dare to believe. An old saying has it that the beginning of philosophy, the beginning of wisdom, is in wonder. In the wonder there is something rather than nothing. In the wonder, for instance, of a newborn baby. Mary felt stirring in her womb the life of God, the Creator become a creature. From the body that God gave to her, she gave to God a body. She looked down into the human face of God, into the face of the one who is, as Christians have said for centuries in the Nicene Creed, "God from God, Light from Light, true God from true God." Miracle of miracles!

And so we say that Mary is the Mother of God, not because of who Mary is but because of who Jesus is. He is true God and true man, and Mary is his mother. As with the two blind men, but on a scale of

Waterhouse, *The Annunciation.*

El Greco, *The Miracle of Christ Healing the Blind.*

cosmic consequence, according to her faith it was done to her. The day predicted by Isaiah has come. Miraculous and true: we are the children of God. Not because of who we are, but because of who Jesus is. He is the Son of God, and we are his brothers and sisters. Looking at us, God the Father sees in us his Son. Because, by faith, the Son of God is in us.

By the gift of the Holy Spirit who creates faith in our minds and hearts, we are embraced in the beloved community that is God—Father, Son, and Holy Spirit. Love requires community, and John the Apostle says in his first letter, "God is love." The Son of God became "Emmanuel, God with us" in order to gather humanity into the eternal life and love of Father, Son, and Holy Spirit. Wonder of wonders!

Jesus asked the two blind men, "Do you believe that I am able to do this?" With them, we say, "Yes, Lord," and he touches us now and says, "According to your faith be it done to you." We know not how, but we know that what needs to be done is being done. According to our faith.

35

*Richard John
Neuhaus*

prayer

Open, we pray you, heavenly Father, our eyes to see and our ears to hear your Word, who is Jesus Christ, true God and true man. As you sent your Spirit upon Mary, so send your Spirit upon us. Embrace us and hold us close within the Trinity of your love, Father, Son, and Holy Spirit. Thus may we, according to your gift of faith, trust the fulfillment of all your promises. Amen. Let it be.

Colombel, *Christ and the Samaritan Woman*.

Scripture: *Isaiah 30:19–21, 23 –26;*
Matthew 9:35; 10:1, 5–8

Richard John
Neuhaus

RECALL ANSELM OF CANTERBURY on how God is beyond our powers to conceive. Anselm's accent is on the *transcendence* of God. Christmas is about Emmanuel, God with us. The accent is on the *immanence* of God. We cannot understand the miracle of the immanence unless we understand the glory of the transcendence. And the other way around.

"In the poorest of the poor we see Jesus in distressed disguise." So said Mother Teresa as she and her nuns ministered to the abandoned babies and dying aged whom they gathered in from the streets of Calcutta. Disguise is central to God's way of dealing with us human beings. Not because God is playing games with us but because the God who is beyond our knowing makes himself known in the disguise of what we can know. The Christian word for this is *revelation*, and the ultimate revelation came by incarnation.

Who would have thought that the baby nursing at Mary's breast is, in truth, the Creator of heaven and earth? Who would have thought that the baby, now a young man, stretched in tortured death upon the cross is, in truth, the King of kings and Lord of lords? Yet some then, and millions upon millions since then, have thought exactly that. God is a master of disguises, in order that we might see. God who is the fullness of Being infiltrated our world of beings in order that we might fully be. Christmas is about incarnation, and incarnation is God's becoming what he is not, in order that we might become what he is. Thus does God reveal himself.

Giordano, *The Good Samaritan.*

The pattern of disguise goes on and on. In Matthew 9, Jesus looks out on the crowds and sees that they are "harassed and helpless, like sheep without a shepherd." All the people of the world are like an abundant harvest, and he tells us, "Pray therefore the Lord of the harvest to send out laborers into the harvest." And the Lord does precisely that through the ministry of his Church.

Many say they admire, even worship, Christ but have no use for the church. But Christ did not give us that option, for the church is the body of which Christ is the head. Head and body cannot be separated. "Lo, I am with you always, to the close of the age," Jesus promised. He is with us, he speaks to us, in and through his church. Which means in and through the people who *are* his church.

To his apostles he said, "He who hears you hears me, and he who rejects you rejects me, and he who rejects me rejects him who sent me." Sometimes it is hard to recognize Christ in the people who are his church, as it is hard to recognize Christ in the poorest of the poor. In both cases, he appears "in distressed disguise." That is the way of incarnation that began at Christmas, the way of the transcendent revealed in the immanent, the way of love that stoops so low to lift so high.

38

Richard John Neuhaus

prayer

Correct our eyesight, we pray you Lord, with the gift of faith that, as we see you in the baby of Bethlehem, so may we see and hear you in those who speak your word, and so may we serve you by serving those in whose distress you are disguised. As at Christmas you came among us to love the unlovable, so teach us to love with the love by which we are loved by you. Amen. Let it be.

history of the feast

A S WE WAIT FOR GOD TO BECOME INCARNATE, we look to the *whole* body of Christ, past and present, for models of embodied faith. The commemoration of saints has been a part of Christian worship since the second century.

Today we remember Saint Nicholas, who was the Bishop of Myra in the province of Lycia during the fourth century. Very little is known about his life, but he is remembered as a man of great faith and compassion. He was also a fierce advocate for those who had been unjustly condemned. But he left behind no writings: the legends surrounding his life are all we have.

Nicholas is most well known in the West as the beloved patron saint of children and gift-giving. His connection to the American character of Santa Claus is faint, but it can be traced. According to tradition, Nicholas' parents died when he was young, leaving him a large sum of money. With his inheritance, Nicholas practiced charity, helping those in need.

One legend in particular illustrates his generosity: a family in his community was desperate; the father had lost all of his money and had been unable to find husbands for his three daughters. The daughters were in danger of being given over to prostitution or another form of degradation when, one night, Nicholas appeared at their home. He tossed three bags of gold into the open window (or down the chimney, in some versions)—thereby saving them from a terrible fate. This tale is probably the source of his eventual connection to the tradition of gift-giving at Christmas.

The custom of giving gifts on Saint Nicholas' feast day probably originated in Europe among Protestants. The Reformation had led many Protestants to all but abandon the remembrance of the saints. But Saint Nicholas remained a popular figure, especially among children, who received gifts in his name on December 6. The custom spread with immigration to North America when Dutch children told their English-speaking friends about "Sinter Klaas," the bishop in red vestments who brought them surprises on his feast day. The American mispronunciation—Santa Claus—eventually took on a life of its own. This jolly Saint Nick also delivered gifts through the chimney, but on Christmas rather than the saint's day. He wore a red suit rather than liturgical vestments, though he still vaguely resembled the old depictions of Nicholas, which showed him with bald head and full beard.

Aside from the obvious disparities between Saint Nicholas and the secular Santa Claus, perhaps the most poignant difference between them can be seen in the nature of the gifts they give. While Santa has his bundle of toys, the gift that Saint Nicholas gives is nothing short of freedom from poverty and desperation. The life of Saint Nicholas is an example of faith made flesh in actions of true charity.

FeasT oF sainT nichoLas
December 6

Scripture: *Luke 6:17–23; John 10*

41

*Richard John
Neuhaus*

S AINT NICHOLAS HAS COME A LONG WAY: from being a fourth-century bishop in the distant Roman province of Lycia, through innumerable pious legends, until he became "Sinter Klaas," which is older Dutch for Saint Nicholas; in our day Americans have turned him into Santa Claus, patron saint of the seasonal commandment to shop until you drop. What should Christians do about Santa Claus? Reject him or reclaim him? I suggest we reclaim him.

Over a hundred years ago, in 1897, a journalist by the name of Francis Church wrote a much-reprinted editorial, "Yes, Virginia, There is a Santa Claus." But of course there isn't. At least not *that* Santa Claus. But there was and is Saint Nicholas, and there is nothing wrong with calling him Santa Claus. For all we know, he may have been a fat man with a big white beard and dressed in red, although he certainly did not live at the North Pole.

The important thing is that he was a holy man. That is why he is called *Saint* Nicholas, for *saint* simply means holy. Now holiness takes many forms. From the stories that Christians told over the centuries, the strikingly holy thing about Nicholas is that he had learned from Jesus what we might call *the law of the gift*. The law of the gift is very simple, although most of us have a hard time learning it and an even harder time living it. The law of the gift is this: the more you give, the more you receive.

Jesus taught the law of the gift in many different ways. For instance, in Matthew 25 he tells the parable of the talents. (A talent was a form of money worth about a thousand dollars today.) One person received five talents, another two, and yet another one. Those who received five

Sienese School, *St. Nicholas of Bari.*

and two talents put them to work, investing wisely, and doubled their money. The master in the parable says to each, "Well done, good and faithful servant." The man with one talent, however, fearfully hung on to what he had been given, lest he lose it, and he ended up losing even what he had. We may take the parable as a lesson in money management, but much, much more important, it is a lesson in how to live.

Richard John Neuhaus

"I came," Jesus said, "that they may have life, and have it abundantly." To live abundantly is to live generously; it is to live the law of the gift. The entire life and mission of Jesus is a gift beyond all expectation. Leaving behind the glory that was his as the Son of God, he gave himself to our sorry human circumstance, even to the point of dying our death on the cross. Having given all, he received all, for he was raised in glory to welcome as his brothers and sisters all who follow him and will live with him forever.

To live the law of the gift means to give of what we have and what we are, and to do so not calculating immediate returns but trusting the promise of eternal reward. Even now we have a taste of that reward as we discover in giving, the key to spiritual greatness, the key to life abundant. That was the greatness, also known as holiness, of Saint Nicholas, whom we know as Santa Claus.

prayer

Liberate us, we pray you, Lord, from the getting and grasping to which we are prone. Teach us the royal way of the law of the gift, that in giving not only things but ourselves we may know even now the life abundant you promise to bring to perfection in eternal life with you. Increase in us gratitude for your gift of yourself, and let that gift of gratitude inspire us to the greatness of living our lives as love in response to love.

Keep ever before our eyes the image of Nicholas and all the saints. Stir us to more daringly follow them in following you, so that, in abandoning all that stands in the way of greatness, we may in abandonment discover life abundant. Forgive us, we plead, our petty excuses for not being saints. Your love for them was no greater than your love for us. Your sustaining presence to them and in them is your sustaining presence to us and in us. You are for us, as you were for them, "Emmanuel, God with us."

From the deepest depth of our hearts, we cry to you, O Lord. No more excuses. Let this Christmas be the time when, at long last, we dare to live the gift already given. Amen. Let it be.

43

Richard John Neuhaus

da Rimini, *The Charity of St. Nicholas of Bari.*

history of the feast

44

"Come, lord jesus." Churches often recite this prayer during the Advent liturgy. But why would we pray for the Lord's coming when he has already been born among us? This is the paradox of the season: advent is a time of tension between the already and the not yet. While we anticipate the coming of Christ in Bethlehem, we also look forward to his second coming at the end of time. The first advent points to the last.

Derived from the Latin *adventus,* the word *advent* means "coming," and refers to all the ways that Christ comes into our lives: past, present, and future. The Latin word is a transliteration of the Greek *epiphaneia,* usually used in reference to the appearance of a king or a queen, or (in pagan times) a god or a goddess. This reminds us that even while we are remembering God's arrival in the flesh of a humble infant, we also prepare for the arrival of the triumphant Messiah, whom prophecy said would be a king.

The purple robes that the clergy wear during this season, while setting a solemn tone, also signify Christ's royalty. All but one of the Advent wreath candles are traditionally purple as well. As we light these candles, we are simultaneously remembering and looking forward to the Incarnation. There is a sense of great expectation: we must make ourselves ready for the appearance of the Lord among us—a vulnerable infant born in a stable, and yet, mysteriously, also a triumphant king.

While we wait for Christ to come in glory, we enter into a sense of expectant hope articulated by the prophet Isaiah. The Scripture readings during the first two or three weeks of Advent concentrate on the promise of God's coming reign, when all creation will live the way God intended. Peace is promised: we read of lions dwelling with lambs and of nations forgiving their grudges. Along with these images of peace come images of justice and judgment.

Christian theologians interpret these Scriptures as prophetic of Jesus: he is the Messiah, the one who was promised. But we are also to understand Isaiah in an eschatological sense—his words speak to God's second advent, when all of these glorious promises will be fulfilled. Clearly our fallen world is still yearning for a savior; all things are not as they should be. During Advent we dwell in that space between the promise and the fulfillment, praying for the Lord Jesus to "come."

Millet, *The Angelus*.

Scott Cairns
second sunday of advent

Scripture: *Isaiah 11:1–10; Psalm 71;*
Romans 15:4–9; Matthew 3:1–12

T HE SLOWEST OF PILGRIMS, I have come to see how my own faith, fragile as it is, is assisted and sustained by the calendar, by the lectionary—by the seasons of the Church. I want to share my growing understanding that our participation in this cycle is one way we might, as they say, *redeem the time*. "The days are evil," writes Saint Paul, imploring us to do something about it. By deliberately attaching our given days to their holy antecedents, we are able to glimpse an eternal significance embodied in our every moment—redeeming our days from what might otherwise be a melancholy emptiness.

During the Advent season, in particular, the eternal significance of our days becomes crucial to our apprehending how, now and ever, God is with us. What is the nature of this gift we have received, this gift we hope yet to receive? Have we come to understand it as a *proposition* or do we welcome it as a *person*? Is the One we call our Lord Jesus Christ a lovely idea or is he the lover of humankind?

For most of my life, I have assumed that each of us must struggle at his or her faith internally, intellectually, and, for the most part, alone. More recently, however, I've suspected that such a solitary journey is nothing short of an aberration—even if it is a very common one—and an aberration that keeps us both divided and conquered. To the extent that we fail to appreciate our connection to—our mutual dependence on—one another, we risk languishing in a faith half-realized, more or less sleepwalking.

This error is in some measure remedied by our observing the common calendar together: the calendar provides daily reminders that Christ

Schongauer, *Adoration of the Child.*

literally walked the earth, and that centuries of his Saints have found his presence available to them at every moment since. In attending to the calendar, I have come to appreciate how Christ and his saints encourage me, not simply by my thinking *of* them, but by my living *with* them—remembering their feast days, recollecting their exemplary lives of prayer, praying to live likewise.

I suspect that the result of this recollection goes beyond a mere commemoration of grace offered in history; rather, the heart of this matter is our subtle liberation from time itself, a sense that, yes, we *commemorate* the Birth, the Baptism, the Transfiguration (and yes! the Death, the Burial, and the Resurrection); we *recall together* those mighty acts of God, which return us and all things to life. More important, we learn to apprehend these events in the present. And better yet, compelling our own bodies to observe the feasts and fasts together, we re*member* the physical presence, the very body of our Lord. We begin to understand that the flesh he becomes is our own flesh. Of a given morning, we may yet apprehend his body utterly near us; of a given morning, we may yet lean into his embrace, accepting that gift, and numberless gifts thereafter.

prayer

As this season of preparation continues, Holy God who is with us, may we lean into every moment of our days to redeem the time, to make the most of our every moment. May we prepare the visible Body of Christ, our community, to receive your eternal approach and your loving embrace. With our faces turned to you, we await your holy descent, and ask, Lord, that you hear our prayer, offered in humility:

49

Scott Cairns

That despite the roar of our days, our hearts might grow still.

That glimpsing the quiet cove, we may seek you in that stillness.

That resting in your presence, our hearts might be prepared to hear you.

That the angel of God might visit the chambers of our hearts.

That the angel of God might say to us, "Rejoice."

That we might hear, and truly respond in joy.

That the angel of God might say to us, "Receive."

That the servant of God might respond, "Let it be as you say."

That our hearts might become fertile wombs in which new life begins.

That we may apprehend the infant life within.

That we might embrace that infant life.

That we may walk with care to bring about new birth.

That we may witness the seed of God bearing Holy Fruit.

As the season of Incarnation approaches, as we prepare to receive Life himself, may we taste and see how our own lives, the life of the world, and the very breath of the universe flow to us from the Holy One made flesh.

Lord, hear our prayer.

Chagall, *The Prophet Isaiah.*

Scripture: *Isaiah 35:1–10; Luke 5:17–26*

Scott Cairns

I RECALL MY FIRST TRIP TO THE HIGH DESERT OF SOUTHERN UTAH, where I'd gone to hike among the red stone pillars of Arches National Monument. I had gone only a little way along the trail—marveling at the enormous spaces that dwarfed me, the immense arches and towers of impossibly red rock, the daunting expanse of Utah's unique, pastel blue sky that seemed endless in its reach—and then I looked down. A flash of vivid color caught my eye, and held it.

I was startled to see the brilliant, deep magenta of a cactus flower just off the trail. The cactus plant itself was unremarkable, except, perhaps, that it was almost completely brown, sun-cracked, wind-bent, and, far as I could guess, nibbled. The plant itself actually seemed more dead than alive; still, from the tip of one scarred, paddle-shaped appendage poured a marvel of brilliant color, a renewal of brilliant life.

And then, having noticed that *one* flower, that *one* burst of color, my eye was thereby led to another flower just beyond the first, and then, just beyond the second, yet another. As I raised my eyes to take in the foreground, I was startled to realize that these brilliant flowers dotted the landscape as far as the eye could see. They had been there all along, but until I had seen the first I'd been oblivious to their presence, blind to their broadcast beauty.

In the middle of his prophecy announcing the regeneration of the earth, the holy prophet Isaiah announces that "the wilderness and the dry land shall be glad, the desert shall rejoice and blossom; like the crocus it shall blossom abundantly, and rejoice with joy and singing." This image is one of *substantial* resurrection; that is, the very *stuff* of a desiccated earth awakens, quickens, blossoms in new life.

Byzantine, *Lowering of the Paralytic through the Roof.*

Today's lectionary also brings us to the familiar story of the paralytic, a man whose body had withered into another sort of desert, whose body was itself devoid of life's energies. This story has, of late, come to suggest to me my own intermittent dryness and paralysis, a bland species of despondency, a nagging sense that the evil in the world—and, frankly, even the occurrences of evil in my own neighborhood—are not to be overcome. This is the sort of paralysis from which I must pray to be healed. Daily.

When I read again how "the man's friends" struggled to place him before our Lord, and when I read again how Christ, seeing the faith of the *friends*, forgave the *paralytic*, I glimpse again his compassion and his power, and I glimpse as well how *corporate* a chore this business of healing may turn out to be. One Body. Of many.

Perhaps my own (our own?) habitual torpor might be healed this season; perhaps, at the appearance of the Word and with the faithful assistance of those who love us, this nagging sense of futility and of powerlessness might be replaced with the faith to rise up, the strength to lift our beds, the willingness to walk. And perhaps Isaiah's words propose as well that the barren desert of human generation will also bloom, and bring to lush fullness the desiccated hearts of humankind. Let us pray that, thereafter, we may become fonts of his love and mercy, that we too may become wells of living water, refreshing those around us, even as we are restored.

prayer

Forever Fresh and Refreshing Source, Living Water, Bright Garment of Dew, descend now and always in one endless, life-bestowing flow. Bring to us those waters that forever quench our thirst. Bring those waters, we pray, to the deserts of our hearts, that from their parched soil, life may spring anew. And more than this, enable that life-giving flow to pour from ourselves to enliven all around us. In the Name of the Father, and of the Son, and of the Holy Spirit. Amen.

SECOND TUESDAY OF ADVENT

Scripture: *Isaiah 40:1–11; Matthew 18:12–14*
(Suggestion: read the Isaiah passage, and wait a bit.)

Scott Cairns

A VOICE SAYS, "CRY!" And so I prepare to lift my voice to cry. But, like the holy prophet, even as I take in breath to make my cry, I wonder, "*What* shall I cry?"

I'm guessing that this must be the unceasing prayer of the prophet; it is certainly the unceasing prayer of the poet. I would suppose that very few poets turn out to be prophets, but what I gather, even so, is that the two share a common *complex of desires*; both are driven *to hear* and *to respond*; both are compelled, that is, *to witness*.

As a poet hovering over the open page, I know in my bones the ache to find the words; I know, as well, the ache of uncertainty about *which* words.

It could be that we all share these complementary desires. We want very much to apprehend God's will, and we hope to respond to it in a way that will please him.

We ache to receive and we ache to give.

Like the prophet, we would seek to comfort his people. We would speak tenderly to those of the holy city, that their warfare might come to an end, that their iniquities and our own might be pardoned. We, too, would "prepare the way of the Lord," had we any clear sense of how that might be done.

In the Gospel according to Saint Matthew, we find a stunning account of the Father's compassion for the wanderer in the wilderness. Jesus asks, "If a man has a hundred sheep, and one of them has gone astray, does he not leave the ninety-nine on the mountains and go in search of the one?" Jesus tells us that "if he finds it, truly, I say to you, he rejoices

Caravaggio, *Adoration of the Shepherds.*

over it more than over the ninety-nine that never went astray. So it is not the will of my Father who is in heaven that even one of these little ones should perish."

Does the answer to our puzzle wait for us here?

Is there a clue here as to what it is that we should cry?

Isaiah writes, "All we like sheep have gone astray. We have turned every one to his own way." For most of us, this isn't exactly news, and it isn't exactly comforting. But Isaiah follows this cry with another: "and the LORD has laid on him the iniquity of us all. He was oppressed, and he was afflicted, yet he opened not his mouth; like a lamb that is led to the slaughter, and like a sheep that before its shearers is dumb, so he opened not his mouth."

That the Shepherd should condescend to become one of the sheep is as appalling now as then. That the God of All should condescend to take on what was, until that moment, all-corrupted flesh is a fearful notion. That *therefore, our own bodies partake of his perfection* is what I now wish to cry aloud, and often as I may.

prayer

Lamb of God and Good Shepherd, Holy Servant and Holy King, Infant Child of the Blessed Womb and Eternal Lord Whom the Heavens Cannot Contain, teach us what we are to cry aloud. Bless our tongues with words that lead us and others truly to the Word. Now and ever, and unto the ages. Amen.

Tanner, *The Good Shepherd.*

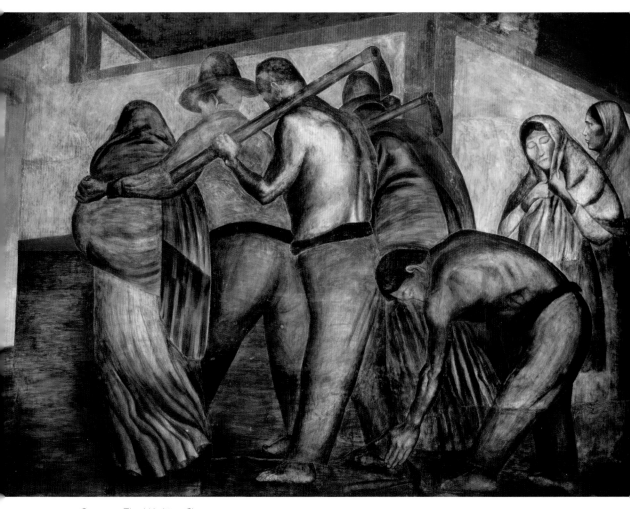

Orozco, *The Working Class.*

SECOND WEDNESDAY OF ADVENT

Scripture: *Isaiah 40:25–31; Matthew 11:28–30*

Scott Cairns

W E PREPARE TO WITNESS A MYSTERY. More to the point, we prepare to witness *The* Mystery, the *God made flesh*. While it is good that we seek to know the Holy One, it is probably not so good to presume that we ever complete the task, to suppose that we ever know anything about him except what he has *made known* to us. The prophet Isaiah helps us to remember our limitations when he writes, "To whom then will you compare me . . . ? says the Holy One."

As you probably already know, all theology—all God talk—comes in one of two particular flavors; let's call them *the way of attributes* and *the way of negations*. The former includes all our propositions of God's *qualities*. The latter provides their necessary *qualification*; it is the tradition that reminds us that *if* God is, say, compassionate, he is not, even so, compassionate in the way a man is compassionate—thank God.

Isaiah's discovery that God is *beyond compare* reveals what may seem a disturbing truth: God is, finally, unknowable. Still, while he is not to be absolutely *known*, he is apparently willing to reveal something of himself to us at nearly every turn. Think of it like this: he cannot be exhausted by our ideas about him, but he is everywhere suggested.

He cannot be comprehended, but he can be touched.

His coming in the flesh—this Mystery we prepare to glimpse again—confirms that he is to be touched.

By his prophets, and by his Word, and by his Holy Spirit, the Father reveals that earthly nature itself—our persons and their surrounding creation—cannot help speaking of the One Who Made Them. "Lift up your eyes on high and see: who created these? He who brings out their host by number, calling them all by name."

Rembrandt, *Head of Christ.*

58

Scott Cairns

In so doing, the Holy One reveals something of his purpose as well. "He gives power to the faint, and to him who has no might he increases strength. Even youths shall faint and be weary, and young men shall fall exhausted; but they who wait for the LORD shall renew their strength, they shall mount up with wings like eagles, they shall run and not be weary, they shall walk and not faint." His taking flesh gives flesh itself a strength and life it did not have before.

Saint Paul tells us that one day he "shall know even as [he] is known." Perhaps he shall. Perhaps *we* shall. Regardless, in the meantime, we *can* know what has been revealed: the Holy One has seen fit to adopt our frailty, so that we might partake in his strength. "Come unto me, all who labor and are heavy laden, and I will give you rest. Take my yoke upon you and learn from me; for I am gentle and lowly in heart, and you will find rest for your souls."

Even his burden is unlike any burden we have known—"For my yoke is easy, and my burden is light"—for it becomes the Light of the World.

prayer

Unknowable One, we stand before you, hardly daring to look up. We offer you our hearts, and pray that we may, this day and ever, worship you in ways that are true. Forgive us those days when we have worshiped false and faulty images we have shaped. Help our frail senses, that we may apprehend your Presence and your Love. In the everlasting Name of the Father, and of the Son, and of the Holy Spirit. Amen.

Scripture: *Isaiah 41:13–20;*
Matthew 11:11–15

59

Scott Cairns

INTO THE DESERT OF HUMAN HISTORY, and even *here*, into the modern deserts we shape and inhabit, at a time when the poor and needy—their tongues parched with thirst—desperately seek life-sustaining waters, the Holy One pours out rivers and fountains. He places the cedar, the acacia, the myrtle, and the olive along their banks, and he sets together the cypress, the plane, and the pine. He is with us in our poverty, and he is with us in our respite from it.

It is good to humbly realize that we are all of us poor, needy, and parched with thirst, just as it is a great relief to discover that he provides all we need and more. Witnessing the bounty and the beauty of his works, we are called to "see and know, [to] consider and understand together, that the hand of the LORD has done this, the Holy One of Israel has created it."

Still, as we prepare our hearts and our homes to receive anew the Gift that supplies all need and more, we must consider and understand together that the deserts we inhabit are to be restored, that while this earth is a means of revelation, it is also more than that. It is an earth, a beautifully, lovingly shaped thing that speaks to us, even as it feeds us, shelters us, holds us up. By his entering our creaturely condition, he makes the stuff itself more worthy.

The Word became flesh and dwelt among us, we say, smiling. So long as we perceive the Word as a reference merely, a stick figure pointing to God, so long as we suppose that all our words are simply signs directing the mind to abstract circumstance, we fail to grasp the appalling, bodily, life-renewing fact of *incarnation*.

Fromentin, *The Land of Thirst.*

He is our help. He takes our hands into his own, and, if we will agree to it, he *makes* our hands into his own, so that we may become the very members of the Body we pray to be.

60

Scott Cairns

prayer   *Only Help of humankind, whose Hand bestows all good, whose Hand both lifts and leads us through the wilderness to his grove beside life-giving waters, O Holy God in whom we live and move and have our being, remember us.*
Both now, and unto the ages of ages. Amen.

Cannicci, *Thirst in the Fields*.

Salome, *The Prodigal Son.*

Scripture: *Isaiah 48:17–19;*
Matthew 11:16–19

63

Scott Cairns

I LOVE THESE LINES IN ISAIAH; the sweetness of their assurance is absolute:

> I am the LORD your God,
> who teaches you to profit,
> who leads you in the way you should go.

And my heart is broken by the verses that follow.

> O that you had hearkened to my commandments!
>   Then your peace would have been like a river,
>   and your righteousness like the waves of the sea;
> Your offspring would have been like the sand,
>   and your descendants like its grains;
>   their name would never be cut off or destroyed from before me.[9]

Would have been is a phrase that makes me wince every time I come across it in the prophets and in the Gospels. This *would have been* is an ongoing reminder how we—individually and collectively, historically and in the present—have missed the fullness of what was given. Had we received his instruction, we and all the world around us would have profited. Had we followed his leading, our *way* would not have led us to a world so torn by intervals of need and greed, so ravaged by cruelty and vengeful responses to cruelty, so divided into self-serving, partisan camps. Had we but hearkened to his commandments, the peace we

Guercino, *The Prodigal Son.*

would know would be an endless flow refreshing our land and ourselves, and our righteousness would be as measureless, powerful, and beautiful as the waves of the sea.

Still, notice the verb tense of those first lines above. Present tense: "I *am* the LORD your God, who *teaches* you to profit, who *leads* you in the way you should go." Evidently, the promise continues even now, despite our historical and present failures to partake of them. Evidently, the hope that we might yet partake of them remains alive. One of the great blessings of growing older (that is, of growing older as a Christian) is a developing awareness of God's continuing mercy, a sweet apprehension that his great mercy is tireless. I say that this is a great blessing, but it has sometimes, even so, caused me to suffer.

My own sins are not as visible as some, nor, perhaps, are they as various. No, my own sins today are pretty much the same sins I've known my entire life. That is to say, throughout my life, I have asked God's forgiveness, repeatedly, for the same, familiar, habitual sins. The suffering in question, therefore, has to do with the chagrin I've often felt in asking to be forgiven, yet again, for the same damned things.

Still, a beloved priest once helped me a great deal with all of this during the sacrament of confession some years ago. Father George Paulsen said to me, "Most of us have been in the same boat. Most of us find that the sins of our days are the sins of our lives. And the worst thing we can do is let our shame *or* our pride keep us from asking forgiveness every time we must." And then he said, "The fact that Jesus will always forgive you finally becomes the prod. One day, you realize that you are tired of this confession, tired of this sin; on that day, you'll decide you *truly* want it gone."

Is Jesus with us? Even as we stammer to name our well-rehearsed sins? Is he with us still? According to the Scriptures, he knew us as we are before he came, and still he chose to come.

Cranach, *Christ and the Adultress.*

65

Scott Cairns

Ever-Merciful God, Compassionate Teacher, Holy One Among Us who leads us now and ever, we lean into your ready embrace, and ask that you revive in us your teaching, that we may this day turn onto the path that we should travel. We ask this in the Name of the Father, and of the Son, and of the Holy Spirit. Amen.

prayer

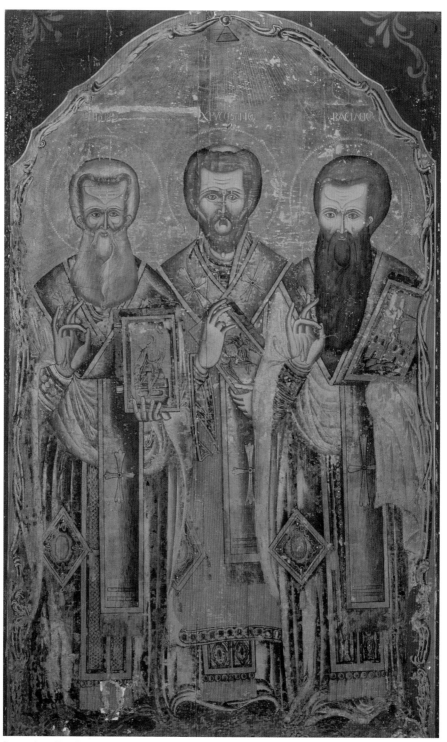

Byzantine, *The Evangelists of Cappadocia: Saint Gregory Nazianus, Saint John Chrysostomus, Saint Basil the Great.*

Scripture: *Sirach 48:1–3, 9–11;*
Matthew 17:10–13

Scott Cairns

AND EVEN NOW THE VOICE CALLS OUT TO US, asking that we turn, bidding us again to prepare the way of the Lord. And most of us, most of the time, will break our hearts trying to respond as we should. *Repentance*—that *turn* of heart and mind—is not so easy to accomplish, nor do our preparations of "the way" ever feel quite complete. Still and always, the voice calls to us from the wilderness and calls us again to attempt these provisional measures.

My own journey along the way has been enabled over the years by many of the men and women we call the desert fathers and the desert mothers—the *abbas* and the *ammas*. They comprise an essential "organ" of Christ's Body; I daresay they are its very heart. They were lifelong pilgrims whose lives were given wholly to prayer and to assisting one another in the path to, as more than one of them has put it, "becoming prayer."

My reading of their *Lives* and *Sayings* has helped me see how repentance itself is far sweeter and far more possible than my prior understanding would have allowed.

Turning away from sin is, without question, one way to apprehend the call to repentance; but I glimpse, even so, in the desert fathers and in writers such as St. Isaac of Syria, St. Gregory of Nyssa, St. Basil the Great, and St. John Chrysostom a healthier characterization of this necessary turn—specifically, that we turn not so much away as toward.

Turning away may diminish our temptation and may diminish our discomfort; it may diminish our awareness of the evil around us, and it nearly always diminishes our awareness of our own culpability in

de La Tour, *Penitent Magdalen*.

that evil. Turning away may even provide the illusion that we are somehow unconnected with those from whom we turn. Whatever its apparent, momentary advantages might be, turning away is precisely what Satan does.

Our specific hope lies in turning toward. As a result, the sin we suffered is behind us just the same, but that sin is no longer the power that occasioned our turn.

We must prepare the way. We must prepare God's path to our hearts, to cultivate an awareness of how near the Holy One bides, how immediately he accompanies our every moment, how beautifully and sweetly he attends our every breath. When we turn toward him, therefore, that change is not so much precipitated by aversion as by love. And look! Love is precisely what has—now and long ago—brought God with us.

68

Scott Cairns

prayer

O Holy One Who Comes, we turn again to you, and we open our hearts, we open our minds, we open our entire beings to your approach. We ask for strength and wisdom that we may now prepare the way. We ask that all may receive you in joy. Now and forever. Amen.

history of the feast

December 8

THE FEAST OF THE CONCEPTION OF THE VIRGIN MARY remembers St. Anne and St. Joachim, Mary's mother and father, who became the grandparents of Jesus. On this day we celebrate Mary's parents, their love for God and for each other, and the loving union that resulted in the conception of their daughter.

The *Protoevangelium of James*, an early Christian text that originated in Egypt during the second century, was consulted by the early church as a source of information about the life of Mary and her parents. According to this work, Mary's conception was the miraculous result of Anne and Joachim's prayers. Having been unable to conceive, they trusted God as the giver of all life. The miracle of Mary's conception by barren parents prefigures the miracle of the Incarnation, God made flesh in the womb of a virgin.

By celebrating the conception of Mary during the season of Advent, we are reminded of the humanity of Christ, who was carried in his mother's womb just as Mary was carried in her mother's womb.

As the angel says in the Gospel of Luke, Mary was "highly favored" or "full of grace." On this day, the church celebrates the grace bestowed on Mary even from the moment of her conception. According to the theologians of the early church, God's plan for the mother of Jesus was that she would be the first among Christians and a model of the church. Therefore we look to her as an example of the redemptive grace that God offers to all of us through his Son. While we are born into a sinful world, this feast day is a reminder that God's grace is always at work in our lives—even at the moment we are conceived.

Christians in the Byzantine church observed the Conception of Mary beginning in the eighth century. The Normans brought the feast to England during the eleventh century, and it later spread throughout Europe. This day was a popular celebration thereafter, long before it became an official feast day of the Roman Church in 1708.

In Spain and other Spanish-speaking parts of the world, the feast of the Conception of Mary is celebrated as Mother's Day. Candles are lit in honor of motherhood, and flowers, flags, and carpets festively decorate homes. Maternity in general is honored on this day, along with the specific maternity of Anne. In this tradition, motherhood itself is aligned with the maternity that brought about the birth of the Son of God; all motherhood becomes a way of experiencing God's presence. In remembering the conception of Mary during Advent, we have a tangible expression of the hope that will be made flesh in the birth of the Savior.

Strozzi, *Education of the Virgin Mary.*

the conception of the virgin Mary

THE THEOTOKOS

December 8

Scott Cairns

Scripture: *Ephesians 1:3–4, 8–9; Philippians 2:2–5*

IN THE EASTERN ORTHODOX CHURCH we speak of the Blessed Virgin Mary most often as the *Theotokos*; she is, therefore, the *God-bearer*. This name—unfamiliar to some—helps to illuminate the mystery of her unique experience. When we say that she bears him, we apprehend that she is both the one who suffers unprecedented, appalling, and unmediated contact with his Holy Presence, and the one who carries his Holy Presence to us. She bears him, and she also bears him to us.

We also say that through her blessed willingness to be "one who hears the word of God and does it," our God became one of us, and so we believe. Within her utterly human womb, the Ineffable One became— cell by cell, knit by knit—a fully human person, initially a human infant drawing sustenance from the mother whose Creator he was, and ultimately the rugged man whose life and death and resurrection bind our lives to his, bind our *life* to his. It is this absolutely bodily fact of our God's incarnation that we seek to apprehend afresh during this and every Advent season. It is precisely this compassionate descent—this bodily arrival of Holy God into the realm of phenomena as one of us— that we hunger to apprehend with greater awareness than, perhaps, we have in the past.

To assist in that greater awareness, on this day we dwell upon the grace by which the human vessel herself was tenderly, beautifully, and graciously prepared. The Theotokos herself was borne by her mother, and born of her mother, but first she came to be—conceived in the lush

Lippi, *The Meeting of Joachim and Anne before the Golden Gate in Jerusalem.*

embrace of two belovéd lovers. This feast day recalls with joy the beauty and mystery of that event.

The Blessed Virgin's parents, "the ancestors of our Lord" Joachim and Anna, are held in high esteem and with great affection throughout the Church Universal—for the love they bore for God. They are esteemed as well for the love they bore for one another; in the East (and increasingly in the West, thanks to Popes John Paul II and Benedict XVI) the purity of their love is in no way diminished by that love's bodily expression. Therefore, their icon (which is also the festal icon of this feast day) shows them holding one another in a tender embrace; in most renditions, they embrace upon their marriage bed.

A hymn of Saint Romanós the Melodist recalls this day:

> Today the bonds of barrenness are loosed;
> for God has heard the prayers of Joachim and Anna.
> And though it was beyond hope, He promised them
> that they would bear a child, from whom would come
> the Immortal One Himself, Who came to be with us.

di Nardo, *The Vision of Joachim.*

prayer

73

Scott Cairns

Beloved Lover of humankind,

Soften our hearts so that we too may have compassion for those who suffer,

so that we too may give gladly of our time and treasure to those in need.

May nothing we do be done in strife, but in confidence and in peace.

May nothing we do be done in foolish pride, but in lowliness of mind let us

esteem others as greater than ourselves.

May we esteem the needs of others as greater than our own.

May we look with kindness and compassion upon their burdens.

May our hearts become as tender wombs prepared to receive your grace, that in

due time may we bring forth the joyful fruit of your Spirit.

May this mind be in us, which was also in Christ Jesus: That being God he

made himself impoverished, and took upon himself the form of a servant,

humbled himself, and was obedient unto death —

yet a death that has brought all to life.

May we suspect our own power to say yes to whatever our God asks of us.

We ask this in the name of the Father, and of the Son, and of the Holy Spirit,

both now and ever, and unto the ages of ages. Amen.

di Nardo, *Birth of the Virgin.*

history of the feast

ON THIS THIRD SUNDAY OF EXPECTATION, we have rounded the corner toward Christmas. Our wait is almost over. But it is still Advent, and the celebration of Christ's birth is yet to come. We rejoice this Sunday not just because Christmas is near—that celebration will come later. The reason for our joy now is based on a more complete understanding of the Incarnation: that we are privileged to experience God with us at all times, even during this sober time of waiting.

In several church traditions, including Roman Catholic, Episcopal, and Lutheran, the third Sunday of Advent is called Gaudete Sunday. *Gaudete* means "rejoice," and is the first word of the entrance song in today's liturgy—*Gaudete in Domino*, or "Rejoice in the Lord."

Joy is also the theme of the reading from Isaiah: "The desert and the parched land will be glad; the wilderness will rejoice and blossom." We are still in the season of waiting and preparation. But Gaudete Sunday represents the joy of God with us even now; it reminds us that our waiting is never without hope. This Sunday we experience anew the essential paradox of the Advent season: light in darkness, presence in absence, fulfillment in the midst of longing.

The paradox of joy in the midst of desire is embodied in a practice involving the Advent wreath. The candles that ring the wreath are traditionally purple in color—all except one. The third Sunday of Advent is represented by a rose-colored candle—a hint of the joy to come. On the other three Sundays we light purple candles, the color of repentance and preparation. But on Gaudete Sunday we get something of a break from our acts of spiritual discipline and receive a foretaste of the grand celebration that will soon take place. Similarly, the clergy are permitted to wear rose-colored vestments on this day. Hints of the Christmas season appear in the use of flowers and the organ, not used in the other Sundays of Advent. In these practices, even the act of waiting is infused with God's incarnate presence.

The familiar Advent song "O Come, O Come, Emmanuel" speaks of Christ's long-awaited coming to Israel, but we should not miss the important point that Christ comes to us again and again, not just in that historical moment in time. Emmanuel means "God with us," and refers to all of the ways that God becomes incarnate in our lives here and now. During Advent, as we remember the day that Christ was born, and as we look forward to the glory of his kingdom, we also come to the profound realization that God breaks into our lives even now.

Scripture: *Isaiah 35:1–6;*
Psalm 145:16, 19; Psalm 130:5

A NTICIPATION LIFTS THE HEART. Desire is created to be fulfilled—perhaps not all at once, more likely in slow stages. Isaiah uttered his prophetic words about the renewal of the natural Creation into a wilderness of spiritual barrenness and thirst. For him, and for many other Old Testament seers, the vacuum of dry indifference into which he spoke was not yet a place of fulfillment. Yet the promise of God through this human mouthpiece (and the word "promise" always holds a kind of certainty) was verdant with hope, a kind of greenness and glory. A softening of hard-heartedness, a lively expectation, would herald the coming of Messiah. And once again, in this season of Advent, the same promise for the same Anointed One is coming closer.

My father, a vigorous preacher and a man of God, was stricken with leukemia in his eighties. In the final weeks of his illness he wrote a farewell letter to all his friends describing his excitement at the prospect of heaven, and of meeting Christ face to face: "I feel like a boy expecting a new bicycle!" He could hardly wait. And yet, of course, though an impatient man, he had to. When he finally died into the light, we grieved, but mostly we were grateful for him and for his release.

Just as in Lent, the season of watchful waiting and preparation for Jesus' dying and the great transformation of his rising, so in Advent, we wait for his coming down to be with us once again. The word *Lent* is derived from the Middle English *lente,* meaning "Spring," and in French "lent" means *slow.* In winter it seems that the season of Spring will never come, and in both Lent and Advent it's the waiting that's hard, the in-between of divine promise and its fulfillment, like a leap

ABOVE: Redon, *The Visitation.*

FACING PAGE: Tanner, *Mary.*

across a ditch after take-off and before landing. Most of us find ourselves dangling in this hiatus, which in the interval may seem a waste of time.

We drum our fingers on the steering wheel as we wait for the light to change. We wait, gnawing with anxiety, for the telephone call that tells us we got the job. For politicians' promises to be fulfilled. For our health to improve. For our headstrong children to grow up. For Jesus to come and resolve the world's confusion and pain.

Paul gives us an astonishing understanding of waiting in the New Testament book of Romans, as rendered by Eugene Peterson, "Waiting does not diminish us, any more than waiting diminishes a pregnant mother. We are enlarged in the waiting. We, of course, don't see what is enlarging us. But the longer we wait, the larger we become, and the more joyful our expectancy." With such motivation, we can wait as we sense God is indeed *with us*, and at work within us, as he was with Mary as the Child within her grew.

Though the protracted waiting time is often the place of distress, even disillusionment, we are counseled in the book of James to "let endurance have its full effect, so that you may be mature and complete." Pain, grief, consternation, even despair, need not diminish us. They can *augment* us by adding to the breadth and depth of our experience, by enriching our spectrum of light and darkness, by keeping us from impulsively jumping into action before the time is ripe, before "the fullness of time." *I wait for the* LORD, *my soul waits, and in his word I hope.*

Luci Shaw

Oelze, *Expectation (Erwartung)*.

prayer

Oh my Lord, keep me from frustration and impatience when I see little evidence of your living and growing in me. Reassure me that waiting time is not wasted time. That your purposes for us all are large and all-embracing enough to hold firm and prevail, no matter the obstacles or distractions. You have told us that "now is the accepted time . . . now is the day of salvation." But perhaps your "now" is different from ours. You see our lives from the infinite perspective of eternity, of kairos. We want immediate action, change, growth in chronos, in "real time." We want to see our problems being resolved. Now.

Help us to realize, as those who love and believe in you, that we, too, are pregnant with Christ by the power of the Holy Spirit, and that day by day we are being enlarged. Augment our hope, widen our imagination, and nourish our anticipation that the astounding fact of "Christ in you, the hope of glory" will turn true in each of us in your good time. Amen.

Dürer, *Saint Christopher Carrying Baby Jesus.*

Scripture: *Numbers 24:2–7, 15–17a;*
Matthew 21:23–27

Luci Shaw

T HE FARMER'S ALMANAC, as well as the long-range meteoro-
logical forecast, may give official-sounding information about
a wet winter in an area of drought, but until the rains fall
and fulfill the prediction, our reasons for belief are based on faith, not
fact. The evidence for a weather prediction or any other authoritative
pronouncement is not in declaration but in demonstration.

There's a spectacular promise given in today's Old Testament reading,
in the prediction in Numbers, spoken, against all odds, by Balaam (the
rebel prophet who resisted the Almighty's plan and was scolded by his
own donkey!). He was not by any means the most reliable forecaster
of the future, nor the most likely mouthpiece for divine authority. But
here it is: "Like stretching palm-groves . . . like gardens beside a river,
like aloes . . . like cedar trees beside the water, water shall flow from
[the LORD's] buckets and his descendants shall have abundant water."
Buckets of water. With today's vast irrigation systems a bucket of water
doesn't sound like much, but in an arid land like Israel every drop counts.
And buckets from God were clearly enough to bring abundance.

There's immense power in small things. An atom. A seed. A word.
Such power is paradoxical. It was the Almighty's supreme authority, and
the power to make that authority effective, that made the paradox of the
Incarnation so stunning—God becoming as small as we are. One of the
three Persons of the Godhead giving up unlimited power (Paul calls it
"emptying" in Philippians 2), becoming downwardly mobile, wordless
for nine months in the womb, a helpless human infant, born in humility
and poverty.

Longoni, *Thoughts of a Hungry Man.*

Lightly as a falling star, immense, may you
drop into the body of the pure young girl like a seed
into its furrow, entering your narrow home under the shadow
of Gabriel's feathers. May your flesh shape itself within her,
swelling her with shame and glory. May her belly grow
round as a small planet, a bowl of golden fruit.

82

Luci Shaw

Again and again Jesus demonstrated this kind of paradoxical authority in his own life. By refusing to be made a king by a momentarily enthusiastic throng. By proclaiming, and acting out the principle, "Whoever wishes to be great among you must be your servant." By his words, which he clearly applied to himself: "Unless a grain of wheat is buried in the ground, dead to the world, it is never any more than a grain of wheat. But if it is buried, it sprouts and reproduces itself many times over."

Buried in a woman's body. Birthed in a cold cave. Buried in a lifetime of ignominy. Buried again in the tomb. Buried in human hearts to be birthed and rooted and risen again—in us. God's buckets of water will do it—drench and nourish the seed in us that makes more seeds—a hundredfold. Balaam would be surprised.

Prayer

Lord Jesus, you gave away your divine power to become enfleshed—one of us. Help us to give away what power we receive from you, that we, though insignificant, may be like showers of refreshing water to those around us. Amen.

THIRD TUESDAY OF ADVENT

Scripture: *Zephaniah 3:1–2, 9–13; Matthew 21:28–32*

Luci Shaw

CONSIDER THE WORDS "SOILED, DEFILED, OPPRESSING"—spoken of God's people—and the human character qualities that follow them in the book of Zephaniah—deaf, obstinate, untrusting, distant. These words express the Almighty's disgust and disappointment that his chosen ones, given multiple opportunities to live in the realm of his blessing, have ignored or despised him.

Now listen to the exuberant contrasts uttered a few verses later about the same people by the same prophet: "The LORD . . . is in your midst, a warrior who gives victory; he will rejoice over you with gladness, he will renew you in his love; he will exult over you with loud singing." The promises are in the future tense, but the reality expressed is voiced with supreme and joyful confidence.

As I was reading this over again, I couldn't help asking myself, "What is different? What has happened to change the whole tenor of the passage? Why does the prophet suddenly turn joyful and begin to enlarge on the relief and excitement he feels? How can he make such a confident pronouncement about the people he has described, earlier in the same chapter, in such contemptuous terms?"

This is a prediction, of course, about future events brought about by the arrival of the Messiah, Jesus, on our planet. It foretells change of an astounding order: "At that time I will change the speech of the peoples to a pure speech, that all of them may call on the name of the LORD and serve him with one accord." The "time" in this case is also mentioned: "Therefore wait . . . for the day when I arise as a witness." Here the old covenant (the promise made to Moses by God, under

Batoni, *The Return of the Prodigal Son.*

which human effort never attained the divine standard) gives way to the new covenant, in which the Father reached down to us to make it possible for us to please him, through the power of the Spirit given. Perhaps Advent began then, in that predictive message, though there was a long delay before Zephaniah's promise began to be fulfilled. And even that in a most incongruous way—in a shabby shed, in an unlikely town, on a bleak, winter night, to a couple with few prospects, with a birth that literally changed the world and all its peoples. Jesus Christ the Son was the Witness to the conquering love of God the Father. In Christ's Advent, the Great Adventure began!

Throughout Scripture the Almighty makes use of similarly striking contrasts to make his point clear. God as Lover is passionate about his people. God as Father cares, as a parent cares about the growth and character of a loved child, about their relationship to him. Contrast has always been one of God's most persuasive teaching tools. Think—if our lives were all milk and honey, contentment and pleasure, a ten on a scale of one to ten, the ten would have no meaning; it would provide nothing to indicate a scale of values. The light seems brighter when it is contrasted with darkness. Relief is heightened when it follows on the heels of despair. The warmth and green of spring are the more welcome because of the bleak cold of winter. And change is possible because Divine Love bridged the gap between his peoples' rebellious pride and depravity and their willing obedience. God is indeed with us!

> *You did the unthinkable.*
> *You built one bridge to us*
> *Long enough, strong enough*
> *to link the unlinkable.*

85

Luci Shaw

Batoni, *God the Father.*

Merciful God, in this Advent season we thank you that you can rewrite the prayer *script of our lives, moving us from wandering to arrival, from self-hatred to acceptance, from distance to nearness, from loneliness to belonging, from weakness to energy, and all this because of the enfleshment of your dear Son, our Lord and Savior Jesus, who became one of us and showed us the way. Amen.*

Buffet, *The Baptism of Christ.*

Scripture: *Isaiah 45:6b–8; 18, 21b–25;*
Luke 7:19–23

87

Luci Shaw

GOD, THE SUPREME AUTHORITY, has spoken since the beginning
of Creation, and continues to speak, in thunder and flood, in
light and darkness, in seasons of rain or drought, in war and
peace. We are bound to listen to his voice, for there is no other. And
because he sent us his Word, and there is no other, our ears must be
open to hear it.

When God speaks the entire world must answer. Some shout, "No!
I won't!" Some complain, "I can't. It's too hard." Some claim personal
autonomy—their "rights." Obeying goes against the grain for many of
us—we rebel at restrictions. Yet some of us, if we are listening, recognize
the voice of loving authority and answer, "Yes."

The natural creation, in all its wildness and profusion, its rich color
and inventiveness, responds to God in seasons, in cycles of birth and
life and death. All creation bears the imprint of his fingers. Pattern and
purpose are visible everywhere. The words "authority" and "author"
have a common root and meaning—they speak of the ability to originate,
to bring into being, and to order that which is thus initiated. As well as
speaking the universe into being, our Creator is the author of beauty,
which we might think unnecessary for practical functioning. But his
attention to colorful detail, his infinite variety of plant and bird and
beast, are indications of grace, as well as additional confirmation that
God is always with us.

The Lord has planted within each of us the esthetic impulse that
allows us to recognize and appreciate that beauty. Created in the image
of a Creator, we are created to create. Who among us has not decorated
a Christmas tree, or an Easter egg, or a living room? Who among us has

From the Luther Bible, Genesis. *Frontispiece Depicting the Creation.*

88

Luci Shaw

not planted a garden, photographed scenery, whistled, sung, danced? I have been listening this afternoon to builders down our street. I hear the antiphon of two sets of hammers ringing their sharp songs as a new house is being erected on an empty lot, and I realize that such construction (rather than destruction) echoes the up-building, creative impulse of God in us. But even builders have to follow the blueprints if the house is to stand firm. God is our Architect, and we are the houses he is building, here in our own Nazareth. The season of Advent reminds us to acknowledge this.

Not only is God the only authority, the One we must acknowledge, to whom we will all bend the knee, he is the One who opens the door to salvation: "Turn to me and be saved, all the ends of the earth! For I am God and there is no other." John the Baptizer and his disciples wondered of Jesus, "Are you the one who is to come, or are we to wait for another?" All Jesus had to tell them, quite simply, was that the blind were seeing, the lame walking, the lepers healed, deaf people could hear, the dead were alive again, and the poor encouraged with good news. Who else but the Promised One in our midst, the God With Us, was capable of such miracles? Later on, Peter had a similar answer to a similar question. He said: "Lord, to whom can we go? You have the words of eternal life."

prayer

Mighty One, as the God who is with us, quench all doubt within us. Reassert yourself to us, in all your creative power and glory. As we remember how your Son gave up that authority to be born and to walk with us on earth, may our love and loyalty rise up to you, strong and certain, to reassure you that we are indeed your creatures. More — we are your sons and daughters. Through Jesus Christ, our Lord. Amen.

Scripture: *Isaiah 54:1–10; Luke 7:24–30*   *Luci Shaw*

WHAT WE *EXPECT* TO SEE may profoundly affect what we actually perceive. We have a God who constantly calls us to pay attention, to observe closely. In the Gospel accounts he often asks, "What are you seeing?" He takes us by the elbow, urging us to "Look! Listen!" as he describes the impact of his messenger, John the Baptizer. Jesus affirms that John is a prophet of strong convictions, a risk-taker not shaken by winds of opinion or circumstance. He's one of the common people, able to live austerely. "He's the one I want you to notice, to listen to," Jesus says. Then, while extolling John's powerful prophetic message, Jesus upends all the old scales of human value. "The least in the kingdom of God is greater than he," he tells the people of his day, and us. In effect he's letting us know that in God's kingdom the valued ones—as he had enumerated earlier in the Beatitudes—are the poor, the hungry, the grieving, the hated and excluded, for their reward "is great in heaven." To us, in our consumer culture, this feels like a huge risk.

Jesus bore out this new, counter-intuitive principle in his own human life. By arriving on this planet in the meanest of circumstances himself he was telling us, "It's the calling of God—and obedience to that call—that matters, not popularity or smooth talk or convenience or great wealth." You can't be very convincing about the need for the good life and its perks if you speak from a stable's muddy floor!

Yet for those who follow him, risking everything, the opportunities are magnificent. Centuries earlier Isaiah had looked forward to a

Bosch, *Saint John the Baptist in the Wilderness.*

time when the disadvantaged (once again, the poor, the barren, the widowed, the diseased) would be encouraged. He spoke to the humble tent-dwellers of his day (and aren't we all temporary inhabitants on this planet?): "Enlarge your tent sites . . . stretch out . . . don't hold back . . . lengthen the tent cords . . . strengthen your stakes . . . spread out to the right and to the left." There's a whole world to be claimed for God! There again, our common perceptions of worth are reversed. The stigma of childlessness and widowhood would be erased.

Too many of us live cautiously, apprehensive about the future, hedging ourselves around with various security systems and insurance programs, paying too little attention to divine assurances of protection. Yet faith always implies risk. We need to remember that we are the creatures of a God who was himself, from our human viewpoint, invested in risky enterprises. Think of the risk of giving human beings free will—the choice for or against God!

Those who witnessed the life of John, the desert-dwelling prophet in his camel-skins, who watched as Jesus, from his birth, was riskily and radically invested in "his Father's business," were given the chance to either accept or refuse the opportunity to become followers of the Son of God. Both risk and faith are expansive and far from passive. They don't say "Maybe," or "Some other time, perhaps." In spite of obstacles they rarely hold back. Lukewarm responses, passivity, will earn us no points on heaven's report card.

Wholeheartedness. That's the quality that should characterize us and that will warm the heart of God.

prayer

Lord, I admit that I often feel inadequate, in spite of your promises. Often I hold back. Help me to take the risks of faith, to be aware of your affirming presence in my life. Now, in Advent, sharpen my spirit and my senses, and enable me to pay attention to the moments of God-radiance when you ask me to look and listen. Amen.

Bagshaw, *Open the Eyes of My Heart.*

Tissot, *Christ Healing the Lepers at Capernaum.*

Scripture: *Isaiah 56:1–3a, 6–8;*
John 5:33–36

93

Luci Shaw

FOR ALL OF RECORDED HISTORY there seem to have been people who didn't quite fit, either because of poverty, or disability, or nationality, or age—those so beaten down by abuse, or struggle, or scorn that they seem paralyzed, without the will to change or be changed. We have come to think of them as outsiders—the hopeless homeless, the alcoholics, the aged, the single mothers, the chronically ill or crippled, whole families dying of famine on parched continents, or decimated by genocide. Have we forgotten that Jesus himself, in his manner of birth, was also a misfit?

Lately I've been reading about the Dalits, the "untouchables" of India—deemed by higher-castes to be the lowest of the low—doomed forever by birth to be the dung-gatherers, street-sweepers, scavengers, butchers, often darker in skin color than members of the higher castes, and with darker lives stretching before them.

I'm also remembering that in the economy of ancient Israel, anyone not of their "chosen" race was forbidden to participate in Hebrew religious rituals, and categorized as Gentiles, foreigners. Outsiders to almost everyone.

Everyone, that is, but God. God promised through Isaiah that he would welcome these "foreigners"—those who loved his name and wished to be part of his family—right into "his "holy mountain," the temple in Jerusalem. Yahweh pledged that he would accept their sacrifices and give them joy as they prayed to him, whereas previously doors had been slammed in their faces. It is in the redeeming nature of God to welcome and reclaim.

Byzantine, *Healing of the Leper.*

Yesterday, I took a ferry to one of the San Juan Islands of Washington. Along the waterfront I noticed groves of one of my favorite trees—the madrona (the *arbutus* to Canadians). I have always felt a special affection for them, with their large glossy green leaves and their trunks that are cinnamon-colored and silky-smooth as a tanned human arm. I love to photograph their bark, which peels off like sunburned skin or house paint, in thin, curling layers. The patterned textures and tones remind me of a kind of natural abstract art.

They also suggest to me an appealing metaphor for acceptance and embrace. When a madrona branch withers and dies, it is not in the nature of the tree to allow it to rot or drop off. Its mother tree refuses to abandon it. Rather, as the young, healthy wood and bark grow, they creep up around the aged gray appendage like a bandage, a second skin, covering and protecting it, welcoming it back to tree-ness. No wonder the word "madrona" means mother.

94

Luci Shaw

Prayer

Forgive me, Jesus, for instinctively shunning those who don't quite fit my preconception of propriety or responsibility. As I gather with others at the stable—shepherds and sages—forgive me for being so absorbed in my own concerns that I ignore the deep needs of others. May your loving, restorative Spirit find a home in me. Show me, today, someone whom I can love and embrace in your name. Amen.

Scripture: *Genesis 49:2, 8–10;*
Matthew 1:1–17

95

Luci Shaw

THE GENEALOGICAL LINE OF JUDAH'S DESCENDANTS given in Matthew's Gospel follows the history of the nation all the way from its father, Abraham, to the birth of Jesus, the fulfillment of all messianic prophecy, the One "who is called Christ." This grand finale is what we celebrate in the weeks of Advent.

The planting of the male "seed," which was to germinate and ripen in the furrows of successive generations, was a vital responsibility as the Jewish nation looked forward to the Messiah, who would be born in that same Judaic line of succession. For every man in this long list there was a woman: a wife, a mother. Yet only five women were named. It is profitable for us to ask *Why?* Why choose *these* five women for particular mention?

Each one, in her own way, was considered seriously flawed. Two of them, Rahab, a Canaanite, and Ruth, of the hated Moabite nation, were aliens. Two of them, Tamar and Rahab, were not only immoral but deceptive as well. Bathsheba and Mary were stigmatized for their presumed sexual activity, Bathsheba as a victim of King David's appetites and Mary as pregnant out of wedlock. All of them were, however, commended for their behavior at critical change-points in their lives. All of them were risk-takers and women of initiative, well fitted, as it turns out, to be part of this stream of humanity as it poured from generation to generation. God's ideas of fitness for his service may not coincide with ours.

Perhaps we may consider this a reminder as to how we may live in our own day. It was Henri Nouwen who made the important distinction

Chagall, *Tamar, The Beautiful Daughter of Judah.*

96

Luci Shaw

between productivity and fruitfulness. Productivity suggests a machine grinding out a commercial product. By contrast, fruitfulness gives us the organic image of a tree, rooted in rich soil, tempered by weather and seasons, by cold and wind and sun, able to give shade, to bud and flower, and to bear fruit.

Years ago a friend of mine who had also lost her husband gave me a magnetic motto for my refrigerator—"Live generatively." It was encouragement to me to be a risk-taker, a "universe-disturber for good." To move in a life-giving direction, not only for one's own sake but for that of others. To contribute to the energy of the world.

Mary, Jesus' mother, lived generatively from the moment of the Annunciation, through pregnancy and childbirth, all the way to her presence along with the disciples in the upper room of Acts 1. Because she said "Yes" to both shame and glory, Jesus, offspring of Abraham and Judah and David, the flower and fruit of her womb, became the Savior of the world.

prayer

Oh my Lord, I long to be fruitful, to know myself growing in likeness to you. Often I feel sterile, not fertile. I need your living water, the sun of your blessing, the wind of your Spirit, the grace of your presence. I yearn to recognize your likeness in my mirror, a reflection that will come only from the daily awareness of "God with me." Amen.

Chagall, *Bathsheba.*

Luci Shaw

history of the feast

THIS IS NOT ONLY A TIME OF WAITING AND PREPARING; it is also a time of joyful anticipation. A sense of expectancy is most deeply felt on the fourth Sunday of Advent—both because we are moving closer to the birth of the Lord and because this Sunday the readings from the Old and New Testaments focus on the coming of the Messiah as fulfilled in the birth of Christ.

Today's reading from Isaiah contains these famous words: "The virgin will be with child and will give birth to a son, and will call him Emmanuel." The prophecy of Emmanuel, God-with-us, comes to pass at the moment when Mary hears the angel's message and conceives Christ. The fourth Sunday of Advent is traditionally the Sunday when the story of the Annunciation is read in church. The archangel Gabriel announces to Mary that she will become pregnant and give birth to the Son of God.

In hearing the Gospel account, we marvel along with Mary at the words of the angel—and we enter the same hope. In our human experience there is no form of anticipation more cherished than that of an expectant mother. As with pregnancy, so with our spiritual lives: the thing anticipated is already forming within us. Along with Mary, our waiting is transformed into an intimately felt presence.

During this week, then, the focus shifts: we begin to prepare for the nativity of Christ. The coming of the Lord is near. Our anticipation is embodied in the liturgy during this final week of Advent in the form of the "O" antiphons. These prayers are traditionally recited beginning on December 17, addressing God by a series of different names such as "O Wisdom" and "O Radiant Dawn." (Each of the antiphons is contained in the hymn "O Come, O Come, Emmanuel.") Each antiphon pleads for God's help and deliverance.

In some traditions the church sanctuary is decorated with greenery at this time. The "greening" of the church sets an atmosphere of growing anticipation of the Lord's arrival.

During the last days of Advent, popular customs around the world also orient our attention to the events immediately leading up to Jesus' birth. The Hispanic tradition of *Las Posadas* is an example of communal preparation for Christ's birth: the whole community re-enacts Mary and Joseph's search for a place to stay. The couple, represented by community members and followed by a procession of children, wander from home to home in the neighborhood, and households refuse to let them in. Knocking on doors, the people sing *Para Pedir Posadas*—the song to request a *posada*—a place to stay. The procession ends at the designated home that finally lets them in. Then begins the celebration in which carols are sung and Scripture is read, especially passages describing Mary and Joseph's journey.

In this final Advent Sunday, we open our doors to the arriving Savior. "God with us" has become a reality in the womb of a young girl. As we attend to the events leading up to Christmas, our sense of anticipation turns to joy.

Kathleen Norris
FOURTH SUNday OF Advent

Author's Note

FOR THE PRAYERS OF THIS FOURTH WEEK of the Advent season, I have employed the traditional "O Antiphons." These brief but potent prayers, which so beautifully weave together all the many themes of Advent, have been used at Vespers at least since the seventh century. Monasteries are among the few remaining communities still singing these antiphons to mark the week beginning December 17 as a special time in the Advent season. Some Benedictine hospitals keep this tradition as well; only in the pediatric ward will you see a Christmas tree before the 17th of December.

Scripture: *Isaiah 7:10–14; Psalm 23;*
Romans 1:1–7; Matthew 1:18–24

As we begin this week, let us keep before us the prayer that begins the O Antiphons :

O Wisdom, O holy word of God,
you govern all creation
with your strong yet tender care:
Come and show your people the way to salvation.

Already sick of Christmas by the time we come to this week, we sometimes feel as if we're in the home stretch of an exhausting race we have no hope of winning. Carols have assaulted us in malls, elevators, and supermarkets for well over a month, and the full-force frenzy

ABOVE: Raphael, *The Holy Family with a Lamb.*

FACING PAGE: Zucchi, *Allegory of the Creation.*

Kathleen Norris

of last-minute shopping, cooking, and family gatherings has yet to begin. In the fourth century, however, Christians were asked to mark December 17 as the beginning of a twenty-one-day period, ending at the Epiphany, in which they focused on the great mystery unfolding in the life of the church, the mystery of God incarnate in human flesh. They were asked to turn away from distraction, from either staying at home and losing themselves in domestic chores, or traveling and being continually stimulated by a change of scenery. Christians were to seek out the church as a place where they could gather as a community not merely to celebrate the birth of Jesus, but to allow the power of the Incarnation to penetrate their lives. How can we even imagine such a thing? How can we make this season holy, when the world tells us that Christmas is over in just a day, and then we rush toward New Year's Eve, and merchants begin putting out goods for Valentine's Day? We might start, presently and simply, by picturing in our mind's eye the great sign prophesied by Isaiah: "Look, the young woman is with child and shall bear a son, and shall name him Immanuel."

This is the genesis of the Christian story, which is also our story. In the iconostasis of some Orthodox churches, the prophet Isaiah is represented by an icon based on this passage, "Our Lady of the Sign." Mary stands, with her arms upraised, palms up, in a gesture of peace. Her womb is depicted as a circle enclosing the Savior, who replicates the gesture. This mother and child embody for us the Wisdom that was with God at the beginning of the world, the Wisdom that moved Moses and the prophets, the Wisdom that is the Word. This is the new genesis, and the new creation, the promise that inspired Paul to say, joyfully, to the Romans that they were called to belong to Jesus Christ, called to be saints.

On this day, we are all inspired to say that God is not distant or inaccessible, but chooses to come into our midst.

Bassano, *The Wedding at Cana.*

103

Kathleen Norris

O sacred Lord of ancient Israel,
who showed yourself to Moses in the burning bush,
who gave him the holy law on Sinai mountain:
Come, stretch out your mighty hand to set us free.

prayer

Chagall, *Moses Before the Burning Bush.*

FOURTH MONDAY OF ADVENT

Scripture: *Judges 13:2–7, 24–25a;*
Matthew 1:18–24

Kathleen
Norris

TODAY OUR READINGS ASK US TO REFLECT ON A MYSTERY: when our lives are most barren, when possibilities are cruelly limited, and despair takes hold, when we feel most keenly the emptiness of life—it is then that God comes close to us. This is a day for those who are grieving or suffering loss during Advent, lamenting that just as we are suffering, and need to weep, the world force-feeds us merriment and cheer. But we are not without hope, for it is because we are so empty, having used the last scrap of our own resources, that God can move in. To work on us, and even to play. Even our bitter emptiness gives God room to play, as at the Creation, placing whales in the sea and humans on dry land, then bringing all the animals to Adam to see what in the world he will call them. This is not a scene of imposed merriment, but of genuine delight and joy.

Today we are reminded that God can fill us, if not with actual children, then with what they represent: a present joy, and hope for the future. We are reminded that Mary is only one of the women in Scripture who bear a child of God's promise. Her ancestors are Sarah, Hannah, and the woman in today's reading from Judges who is known only as the wife of Manoah and mother of Samson.

Just as God's promise that Manoah's wife would bear a son was fulfilled, God's vow—"I will be with you"—was fulfilled in Mary. But this promise was also revealed in Joseph's great righteousness and mercy. He was not willing to expose this young woman to public disgrace, condemning her to a lifetime of being despised and poor, a social outcast, perhaps even forced into prostitution or exile. A woman

Crespi, *The Dream of Saint Joseph.*

without a man to look out for her was the most vulnerable of people, as is still the case in many cultures today. But Joseph quietly took Mary as his wife, and accepted the mystery of her unborn child.

Today we thank the God who sees and is angered by the injustice and oppression that people impose on one another. And we gratefully envision what Jeremiah foresaw thousands of years ago: "The days are surely coming, says the LORD"—let that note, surely, ring out like a bell!—when a ruler who brings justice and righteousness in his wake, will lead us not merely out of Egypt, but out of our slavery to sin. Having conquered even death, he will take us back to our true home, to live eternally in God's presence.

The promise of Isaiah that we heard at the beginning of Advent is now closer to fruition, if we will only pay attention to the signs: "The wilderness and the dry lands shall be glad, the desert shall rejoice and bloom." Now, as the world clamors for more toys and loud festivity, is the time for us to put first things first, and seek silence, if only for a few precious minutes a day. Now is the time when, ever more intently, we are to watch and listen for God.

106

Kathleen Norris

prayer

O Flower of Jesse's stem,
you have been raised up as a sign for all peoples;
rulers stand silent in your presence;
the nations bow down in worship before you.
Come, let nothing keep you from coming to our aid.

Scripture: *Isaiah 7:10–14;*
Luke 1:26–38

107

Kathleen
Norris

ISAIAH'S PROPHECY OF LAST SUNDAY RINGS OUT AGAIN TODAY: "the young woman is with child and shall bear a son, and shall name him Immanuel." But we are farther along on our Advent journey, drawing closer to the true meaning of Isaiah's words. We hear them fulfilled in today's Gospel, the Annunciation of the good news to Mary.

Surely the story sounded less than good to Mary's ears, and even frightening. Who is she, a peasant girl, that an angel of God should appear before her? Who is she, to bear the Savior God promised to Israel? Why should this great blessing, and burden, come into her humble life? Unlike Zechariah, however, Mary believes. For her question to the angel is not, "How will I know?" but, "How can this be?" She has already accepted the truth of what the angel tells her.

But Mary still has to assent to it, to answer "Yes." And on that our salvation hinges. Will the door open, or remain locked? Will we be subject to evil and death forever, or be led out into freedom? The answer depends on Mary, and it depends on us. As Denise Levertov writes in her poem "Annunciation,"

> Aren't there annunciations
> of one sort or another
> in most lives?
>
>   Some unwillingly
> undertake great destinies,
> enact them in sullen pride,
> uncomprehending.

Blake, *Zacharias and the Angel.*

More often
those moments
when roads of light and storm
open from darkness in a man or woman,
are turned away from
in dread, in a wave of weakness, in despair
and with relief.
Ordinary lives continue.
God does not smite them.
But the gates close, the pathway vanishes.

The questions God asks us are always questions of being, rather than of knowing. And simply recognizing those moments, stopping for a moment because something, or someone, wants our attention, can matter. Chances are, we will not see or hear an angel—and if we do, beware; remember the desert monk who defeated a demon that appeared before him as an angel of light, by saying, "I haven't done anything to deserve an angel!" But it will be clear that we are being asked to say either "Yes" or "No," to embrace or ignore what God has set before us.

Like the ancient Israelites in the desert, we can long for the security of the world we knew in Egypt. Slaves, after all, have the security of knowing their place in the world. Or, like Mary, we can say "Yes" to the new, uncertain reality that promises true freedom. Saying "Yes" to God will always mean more than we can possibly imagine, both for us, and for others. Walls and stumbling blocks that seemed impassable crumble suddenly, as we let our fears go. Like Mary, we have no way of knowing any of this. We can ask for courage, however, and trust that God has not led us into this new land only to abandon us there.

109

Kathleen Norris

Bramley, *A Hopeless Dawn.*

O Key of David, O royal power of Israel,
    controlling at your will the gate of heaven:
Come, break down the prison walls of death
    for those who dwell in darkness and the shadow of death,
        and lead your captive people into freedom.

PRAYER

El Greco, *The Annunciation*.

Scripture: *Song of Solomon 2:8–14;*
Luke 1:39–45

Kathleen
Norris

A N INDELIBLE IMAGE: two pregnant women, one of them just beginning to show, the other round and heavy, who is startled when her infant leaps in her womb. It's a joyful scene, both everyday and extraordinary. For Elizabeth's child, we are told, recognizes that Mary bears the Savior long promised to Israel. Mary is, as Elizabeth suddenly exclaims—no doubt after being kicked hard by John—the mother of the Lord. It usually takes a good kick for us to recognize that God is in our midst.

Yet for all its gentle comedy and joy, this scene strikes a solemn note. For we, the hearers of this story, know that these two, like all pregnant women, are destined to give birth to human beings who will one day die. This is the heroism of motherhood. We also know that their children are destined for martyrdom, and that Mary will witness her son's agonizing death on the cross. Like any one of us, Jesus is subject to pain and suffering. He will face his own mortality in the garden of Gethsemane.

In some churches, during Advent, pillars are decorated with wreaths that resemble a crown of thorns. I love the way this causes me to remember that, in this life, true joy is never perfect, but comes admixed with pain and suffering. Whatever God has brought us into this world to do, we cannot do it without sacrifice. The traditional Advent wreath, of course, is plump with greenery and promise. In *To Dance With God*, Gertrud Mueller Nelson wonders if its origins lie in the ancient European custom of marking the winter solstice by removing the wheels from farm carts and wagons. Stripped of all utility, the wheels were then brought indoors and decorated: color and candles to celebrate light in the dark of winter, and to remind the sun to return.

Fra Angelico, *The Annunciation.*

112

Kathleen Norris

Today, as in all of Advent, we are asked to set mere use and purpose aside, and fathom the depths of existence. Dawn emerges out of night, and the first cry of life comes from the pain of childbirth. Only through the Cross is our new life revealed. Only out of the hard ground of winter can new life come.

Today, in the Song of Solomon, we hear the words of God's beloved, who would love us as well: "For now the winter is past, the rain is over and gone. The flowers appear on the earth." This is the voice that John responded to from inside his mother's womb, and the voice that calls to us, weak as we are, imperfect, and wracked with the pain of sin and death. Still, God calls to us, saying, "Let me see your face, let me hear your voice; for your voice is sweet, and your face is lovely."

prayer

O radiant Dawn,
splendor of eternal light, sun of justice:
Come, shine on those who dwell in darkness
and the shadow of death.

fourth thursday of advent

Scripture: *1 Samuel 1:24–28;*
Luke 1:46–56

Kathleen
Norris

WE ARE FORCEFULLY REMINDED in the readings that, even as we gather with our loved ones to celebrate Christmas, Christ did not become incarnate only for our small circle, but for the welfare of all humanity, and for the whole of creation. Today is a day to ask ourselves what we have done with all God has given us. When our prayers are answered, as was Hannah's, do we stop to give thanks? Do we, like Hannah, take the next step, and recognize that what God gives to us we must give back to the Lord in service to others?

Just as surely as Zechariah has lost his voice, today Mary finds hers. After Elizabeth exclaims, "Blessed is she who believed that there would be a fulfillment of what was spoken to her by the Lord," the Gospel continues, simply, "And Mary said," giving us little sense of what is to come. For Mary utters a song so powerful that its meaning still resonates in profound and disturbing ways. In the twentieth century Mary's "Magnificat" became a cornerstone of liberation theology, so much so that during the 1980s the government of Guatemala found its message so subversive that it banned its recitation in public worship.

The Magnificat reminds us that what we most value, all that gives us status—power, pride, strength, and wealth—can be a barrier to receiving what God has in store for us. If we have it all, or think we can buy it all, there will be no Christmas for us. If we are full of ourselves, there will be no room for God to enter our hearts at Christmas. Mary's prayer of praise, like many of the psalms, calls us to consider our true condition: God is God, and we are the creatures God formed out of earth. The nations are but nations, and even the power of a mighty army cannot save us. We all return to dust. And if we hope to rise in

Pontormo, *The Visitation.*

God's new creation, where love and justice will reign triumphant, our responsibility, here and now, is to reject the temptation to employ power and force and oppression against those weaker than ourselves. We honor the Incarnation best by honoring God's image in all people, and seeking to make this world into a place of welcome for the Prince of Peace.

114

Kathleen Norris

prayer

O Ruler of all the nations,
the only joy of every human heart,
O Keystone of the mighty arch of humankind:
Come and save the creature you fashioned from the dust.

Walker, *Light Manifest.*

FOURTH FRIDAY OF ADVENT

Scripture: *Malachi 3:1–4, 4:5–6;*
Luke 1:57–66

*Kathleen
Norris*

THE PROPHET MALACHI, chosen in church tradition to conclude the Hebrew Scriptures, has for us today both a blessing and a warning. Yes, the Lord we seek will come, suddenly, to his temple. "The messenger of the covenant in whom you delight—indeed he is coming, says the LORD of hosts. But who can endure the day of his coming, and who can stand when he appears?"

This passage is echoed in the Revelation to John, when the angel opens the sixth seal, and all who have trusted more in their own strength and wealth than in God—"the kings of the earth and the magnates and the generals and the rich and the powerful, and everyone, slave and free"—flee in terror to caves and hide among rocks. They call to the mountains, "Fall on us and hide us from the face of the one seated on the throne and from the wrath of the Lamb; for the great day of their wrath has come, and who is able to stand?"

The infant Jesus who comes at Christmas is much easier to welcome than the one crucified at Calvary. And even less so, the one who will come at the end of time, the risen Lord returning, suddenly, and without warning. When this Jesus comes to find us, our first instinct is to hide. Who can endure his anger over what we have done to the creation, to each other, and to ourselves?

It helps to ask ourselves the question Jesus so often asks the disciples: "Why are you afraid?" It helps to recall the burning bush God set before Moses, for God's fire did not destroy it. If we truly trust in God, we find more assurance than terror in the thought that God wants to purify us, so that everything evil in us turns to ash, and only the good remains.

van Dyck, *The Savior of the World.*

God's just anger is a refiner's fire: to suffer it is not a gentle thing, but the end result is pure beauty.

Today's Gospel tells of Elizabeth giving birth, and Zechariah speaking again, his voice restored as quickly and mysteriously as it was silenced. Both mother and father stun their relatives by insisting, against the well-established custom of using names from within the family, that this child is to be called John. This seems a small thing today, when children are sometimes named after characters in soap operas, but at the time it was enough to be talked about throughout Judea. It was enough to induce fear. This child was named by God, and it does not go easy for those who are so touched by God's hand. "What, then," the people wondered, "will this child become?"

I hear, in that question, a restating of Malachi's truth. The Lord we desire may indeed be close at hand, but it will not be easy for us to accept his call. If we continue reading in the Gospel, we find the song that Zechariah sings in praise of God, called the "Benedictus" in church tradition, and commonly recited at Morning Prayer. In this song, we find that it is not merely John the Baptist, but we ourselves who are addressed: "And you, child, will be called the prophet of the Most High; for you will go before the Lord to prepare his ways, to give knowledge of salvation to his people by the forgiveness of their sins."

This was John's calling, and it is our own, a truth both consoling and terrifying. We are enslaved, by selfishness and addiction and all the wreckage that sin can wreak on the world, but are we willing to risk being freed? Do we dare to enter that dangerous new country, leaving sure comforts behind? Perhaps it is time to surrender, open our hearts, and accept the wonder of Christmas by saying, with Karl Rahner, "We have no choice. God is with us."

Dürer, *The Virgin in Prayer*.

117

*Kathleen
Norris*

*O Emmanuel, ruler and lawgiver,
desire of the nations,
savior of all people:
Come and set us free, Lord our God.*

prayer

history of the feast

December 24

CHRISTMAS EVE is the beginning of the feast of the Nativity, the celebration of God with us. All of the waiting and preparation of Advent leads us to this night. On the evening before the celebration of Christ's birth, the church gathers for a vigil. Images of darkness and light suffuse our worship during the Christmas Eve liturgy: we are entering into the dark night of our Savior's birth, when Light will come into the world.

With awe and joy we approach the manger in Bethlehem, as did the original visitors to the stable. This scene is often enacted in the setting out—in a church or public place—of the crèche. A crèche is a nativity scene that displays images of the manger and those who journeyed to see the newborn Savior. The term *crèche* refers both to the stable where Jesus was born and to the manger in which he was laid. In the early church many Christians made a pilgrimage to the place in Bethlehem where, according to tradition, Christ was born. Then during the sixth century, a crèche was built at the church of St. Mary Major in Rome, beginning the tradition of decorating a manger in the days leading up to Christmas.

Today churches often incorporate a crèche into their Christmas worship by displaying nativity scenes and enacting traditional nativity plays. The Christmas pageants many of us grew up with as children actually have their origins in the medieval "mystery plays" sponsored by a town's craft guilds and played out in the squares of town and village.

Francis of Assisi, who had a manger built in Greccio, Italy, for Christmas of 1223, helped to popularize the use of the crèche outside of the liturgy. In French homes, it is traditional for children to follow a custom of preparing a crèche in the days leading up to Christmas. For each prayer or act of kindness that they perform during the season, they place a piece of straw in the manger. With each token of straw, the children are preparing the place for Christ to be born—literally, by creating a soft bed of straw, and also figuratively, by preparing their hearts with acts of kindness and prayerful devotion.

The custom of preparing the crèche mirrors the act of Christians preparing their hearts for the arrival of Emmanuel, God with us. On this night, the eve of the Nativity, we open our hearts to receive the gift of the Christ child, born among us. All through Advent and now on this first night of the Christmas season, we ourselves become the manger, inviting Christ to dwell within us just as he found rest in that Bethlehem stable.

Scripture: *Isaiah 62:1–5; Psalm 88;
Acts 13:16–17, 22–25; Matthew 1:1–25*

121

*Kathleen
Norris*

A WOMAN I KNOW, whose family owns a retail business in a small town, once commented, "Christmas is not a pleasant time at our house." I found this a sad commentary on what Christmas has become for so many of us: a time of increased anxiety and stress and discord. We lash out at loved ones because we're spending money we can't afford to spend, or, as with this woman, because Christmas is what makes or breaks our family's livelihood for the year.

What a mess we have made of God's greatest gift to us! We scurry for weeks, baking, shopping, working extra hours, rehearsing and presenting Christmas pageants. Then, on the eve of the Nativity, we force our frantic, over-stimulated children into their "best," most uncomfortable clothes, and we all rush off to church where we collapse into a pew. If we're lucky, we think, we can nod off listening to the lengthy recitation of Jesus' genealogy that opens the Gospel of Matthew. After that, it's playing Santa, and confronting those maddening "some assembly required" directions until the wee hours.

By Christmas Eve, most of us find ourselves very far from our true reasons for celebrating, reasons that are so eloquently expressed in the processional of the Christmas Vigil in the Byzantine rite: "Rejoice, Jerusalem! All you lovers of Sion, share our festivities! On this day the age-old bonds of Adam's condemnation were broken, paradise was opened for us, the serpent was crushed, and the woman, whom he once deceived, lives now as mother of the creator."

ABOVE: Munch, *Anxiety.*

FACING PAGE: Turner, *Shade and Darkness.*

Here, in just a few simple words, is the essence of Christmas. It is not merely the birth of Jesus we celebrate tonight, although we recall it joyfully, in song and story. The feast of the Incarnation invites us to celebrate also Jesus' death, resurrection, and coming again in glory. It is our salvation story, and all of creation is invited to dance, sing, and feast. But we are so exhausted. How is it possible to bridge the gap between our sorry reality and the glad, grateful recognition of the Incarnation as the mainstay of our faith? We might begin by acknowledging that if we have neglected the spiritual call of Advent for yet another year, and have allowed ourselves to become thoroughly frazzled by December 24, all is not lost. We are, in fact, in very good shape for Christmas.

It is precisely because we are weary, and poor in spirit, that God can touch us with hope. This is not an easy truth. It means that we accept our common lot, and take up our share of the cross. It means that we do not gloss over the evils we confront every day, both within ourselves and without. Our sacrifices may be great. But as the martyred archbishop of El Salvador, Oscar Romero, once said, it is only the poor and hungry, those who know they need someone to come on their behalf, who can celebrate Christmas.

Tonight we are asked to acknowledge that the world we have made is in darkness. We are asked to be attentive, and keep vigil for the light of Christ. The readings are not particularly comforting. Psalm 88, a lament which is also commonly read on Good Friday, is stark in its appraisal: "For my soul is full of troubles, and my life draws near to Sheol," the underworld of the dead. The passage from Acts asks us to consider that, just as Israel needed God to lead them out of Egypt, so we need Christ to lead us out of our present slavery to sin. We, and our world, are broken. Even our homes have become places of physical and psychological violence. It is only God, through Jesus Christ, who can make us whole again.

The prophecy of Isaiah allows us to imagine a time when God's promise will be fulfilled, and we will no longer be desolate, or forsaken, but found, and beloved of God. We find a note of hope also in the Gospel of Matthew. In the long list of Jesus' forbears, we find the whole range of humanity: not only God's faithful, but adulterers, murderers, rebels, conspirators, transgressors of all sorts, both the fearful and the bold. And yet God's purpose is not thwarted. In Jesus Christ, God turns even human dysfunction to the good.

The genealogy of Jesus reveals that God chooses to work with us as we are, using our weaknesses, even more than our strengths, to fulfill the divine purpose. At tonight's vigil, in a world as cold and cruel and unjust as it was at the time of Jesus' birth in a stable, we desire something better. And in desiring it, we come to believe that it is possible. We await its coming in hope.

123

Kathleen Norris

prayer

O God, who spoke all creation into being:

When you created human flesh, we betrayed you by our disobedience.

When you led us out of slavery in Egypt, we doubted and defied you.

Yet you chose to come among us through your Son, Jesus Christ,

who suffered death on our behalf, putting an end to the power of sin and death.

For this great gift of your steadfast love, we give you thanks.

Help us, O Lord, to keep vigil this night.

Help us to watch for the signs of your coming into our midst, not in the splendid palaces of power, but in hearts humbled by need.

Help us to believe that the darkness of cruelty and sin will never overcome the light, and the mercy, of Christ.

Help us to endure, knowing that the evil and injustice of this world cannot prevail against your Word.

We ask this in the name of your Word made flesh, our Savior, Jesus Christ. Amen.

CHRISTMAS DAY IS THE FEAST OF THE INCARNATION, the celebration of God with us. That which we have longed for has entered our human experience. In Christmas services, we hear the pronouncement of the angel: "I bring you good news of great joy that will be for all the people. Today in the town of David a Savior has been born to you; he is Christ the Lord."

Families and churches often represent the Incarnation visually on Christmas by lighting the "Christ candle" in the center of the Advent wreath. In some churches, the Gospel is read from the center of the church on this day, rather than from the lectern—symbolizing the presence of God, the Word made flesh, in our midst.

The celebration of the Nativity of Our Lord probably originated in Rome during the fourth century. Up until then, Christians had commemorated Christ's birth, along with other important events related to his early life, on January 6, the feast day of Epiphany. (In many of the Eastern churches—such as the Russian, Greek, and Serbian—Christmas is still celebrated on January 6 or 7, preserving this ancient observance.)

The first mention of December 25 as the day of Christ's Nativity appears on a Roman calendar that was prepared in the year 336. Some theories suggest that the date was chosen to counter the pagan festival of the birthday of the sun, celebrated on the same date during the winter solstice. Others suggest that December 25 was chosen by counting nine months from the traditional date of Christ's conception, March 25. Either way, it is clear that the church saw a need to commemorate the birth of Christ on its own holiday, emphasizing the unique importance of the Incarnation event.

On Christmas, we celebrate the mystery of humanity and divinity becoming one. The early church theologians stressed that the Incarnation should not be seen as condescension, as the "descent" of God to man, but as the lifting up of humanity into the divine life. As the ancient creed of St. Athanasius puts it, Christ is both divine and human "not by conversion of the Godhead into flesh, but by taking of that manhood into God."

The Incarnation makes it possible for the redeemed life to be lived out in this flesh, on this ordinary earth. The Nativity ennobles the lowliest aspects of everyday life: God chose to be born in a stable, with animals and shepherds as his first visitors. In this lies the power of the Incarnation: the humblest things are the most exalted.

The liturgy on Christmas rings out with joy. Carols are sung, often with the aid of trumpets, trombones, and other festive instruments. Incense fills the church, and clergy change their vestments to white or a festive red. In some churches liturgical dance adds to the atmosphere of rejoicing. And the Gloria, which had been omitted during Advent, makes its triumphant return. Just as "Glory to God in the highest" was the song of the angels who appeared to the shepherds on the night of Christ's birth, so it becomes our song as we enter the Christmas season.

And we are entering a new season. For the commercial world, Christmas ends at midnight tonight, followed only by retail sales. But in the liturgical calendar this day is just the beginning of the Christmas season—a celebration that will continue for twelve more days, until the feast of the Epiphany.

THE NATIVITY OF OUR LORD

December 25

Scripture: *Isaiah 52:7–10; Hebrews 1:1–6;*
John 1:1–18

Kathleen
Norris

How beautiful upon the mountains
are the feet of the messenger who announces peace,
who brings good news,
who announces salvation,
who says to Zion, "Your God reigns."
—*Isaiah 52:7 (NRSV)*

OUR VIGIL ENDS WHEN, like the watchmen of ancient Israel, we sing for joy at our Savior's coming. On this day, the full dimension of our relationship with God is revealed and we become, through Christ, God's children. Because God took on human flesh, human flesh is made holy. Even lowly and dusty feet, if they carry God's message, are beautiful. This is the glory, and the scandal, of the feast we celebrate today. Things that we would prefer to keep separate— the holy and the profane—have come together, in a cold and smelly stable. The God of Ages is warmed by the breath of cattle, and by his mother's arms.

Our minds revolt at the thought. But today, as Thomas Merton wrote, "eternity enters into time, and time, sanctified, is caught up into eternity." Time, ourselves, and all of nature, are now made holy, illuminated by Christ. All that exists has the potential to reveal God's truth and love.

We celebrate today God's doing a new thing with an ancient creation. God created us in his image, but we betrayed this gift in Eden. Today, we give thanks that the Nativity of Jesus has renewed it in us. Today

ABOVE: van Dyck, *Nativity.*

FACING PAGE: Giotto, *Nativity.*

is the day when, as the great early church poet Ephraem of Syria says, "The creator of all things became the restorer. He gave them back their former beauty."

Today we are asked to sing the new song that we will hear again at the end of time. Although our celebration of Christmas is festive indeed, we know that it is not the perfect feast to come. As Judea suffered under the yoke of empire, so millions suffer today under the yoke of unjust economies. The poor labor for pennies a day and die in misery when they are no longer of use; the rich consume compulsively, imprisoned by the notion that their worth as human beings comes from social status and possessions.

On Christmas, of all days, we are not to forget that too many families are homeless, too many children die of starvation and treatable disease, or that too many people are victimized by a profitable weapons trade that fuels genocidal conflict and terrorist acts around the world. How can we celebrate Christmas in such a world? The answer is that the joyful feast of Christmas exists because, and in spite of, the pitiful human condition.

We might take Joseph as our model in rejecting any temptation to despair. In icons of the Nativity he is set in a bottom corner, his hands on his head in a posture of resignation. The devil, depicted as a little man covered with hair, is trying to convince him that there is nothing extraordinary about this child, nothing changed about the world at his birth.

Today, we insist that everything has changed, and that it is good. We rejoice that God has come into our world, in human flesh, and we believe that Christ will come again. We give thanks for the Christ we know now, in the poor and oppressed and despairing of this world, and we believe that we will know him also when he comes in glory. Today, we are not resigned; we stand up and sing, for God has not given up on us. We are his own, and we are welcomed to the feast.

Boucher, *The Nativity.*

128

Kathleen Norris

Giver of all that is good,
we thank you today for the gift of your Son, Jesus Christ, our Lord,
who was born into poverty in a hard and cruel time,
who gave himself for us,
and lives with you in glory.

We thank you for all your friends and prophets who have gone before us,
and those who taught us to celebrate this feast of the Nativity with beloved
Scripture, and beloved carols, and loud rejoicing;
help us to teach those who come after us that Christmas is a holy time, a
time to seek reconciliation and peace.

Bless us, Lord, as we seek Christ in the lowly mangers of this world,
bless us, as we seek to honor the mystery of the Incarnation in our midst,
remembering always that you made us, and all humanity, in your divine
image.

Help us to gladly welcome today, and all days,
your Wisdom, your Power,
your Emmanuel, your Prince of Peace.

history of the feast

THE DAY AFTER CHRISTMAS is set aside as a memorial of Stephen, the first Christian martyr. Once again, the church seems to take a counter-intuitive approach, reminding us of sin and suffering hard on the heels of the joyful celebration of the Nativity.

But it is possible to see the reason behind this decision. In Advent we were reminded that our longing for the light of Christ is conditioned by the darkness that often surrounds us. In remembering Stephen on the second day of Christmas, the church contemplates the link between life and death, between Christ's incarnation and his crucifixion.

Even at the moment of his birth, Jesus is headed toward a sacrificial death, a fact foreshadowed by the gifts of the Magi. Along with gold and frankincense, gifts suitable for kings and priests, these men bring the newborn baby myrrh—the ointment used to prepare bodies for the grave.

As Jesus says in the Gospels, there is no greater love than the willingness to lay down one's life for a friend. From the very beginning, this has been a stark reality for many of Christ's most faithful friends.

We learn about Stephen in the Acts of the Apostles. Stephen was a Greek Jew and one of the first deacons of the church, having been appointed by the apostles to minister to the needy in his community. In his working with the poor, Stephen was filled with "God's grace and power" and performed "wonders and miraculous signs among the people."

Stephen not only performed miracles, but he also preached against the notion that God dwelled only in the Temple—a claim that earned the suspicion of Jewish authorities. He was brought before the Sanhedrin, where false witnesses accused him of trying to break the customs regarding worship handed down in the laws of Moses. Stephen defended himself, demonstrating through his interpretation of the Old Testament Scriptures that the law was fulfilled in the person of Christ. God, he said, dwells not only in temples built by human hands, but also within human hearts.

The reaction of the authorities was an attempt to stifle this radical message that God is with us—and within us. They gnashed their teeth and literally covered their ears. When Stephen wouldn't stop talking, they dragged him out of the city and stoned him to death.

In the life and death of Stephen, we perceive another facet of the Incarnation. God became incarnate in a human body in order that—after his death and resurrection—he can be made flesh once again in the actions of his followers. We are, in the words of the apostle Paul, the body of Christ. And there are times when members of the body are called to make the ultimate sacrifice, as Stephen did.

The Christians who made this day a commemoration of Stephen's martyrdom were not sentimental, but neither were they without hope. They believed that we should celebrate our redemption, but never forget its cost.

Carracci, *The Stoning of Saint Stephen*.

Scripture: *Acts 6:8–10, 7:54–59;*
Matthew 10:17–22

W E OFTEN THINK THAT WHEN DECEMBER 25 IS PAST, Christmas
is over. But no, this rich, extended feast is just beginning.
The whole of Christmas—all twelve days of it—is about the
Incarnation. This central mystery of Christian faith is brought home to
us by the infant in the manger, the Child wrapped in swaddling-clothes.
The cradle scene stays with us—or at least, it is supposed to remain set
up—throughout the twelve days. Gazing on the scene of the Nativity is
one way to grasp the Incarnation vividly, completely.

Another way is to relate this mystery to some personal experience.
For me, the Incarnation becomes vivid when I recall my own experience
of childbearing. I was so eager to be a mother, so much waiting for
good news; I was awed and pleased when I first learned I was pregnant:
it felt like a visitation from an angel.

Over nine months of waiting I was sometimes exalted, sometimes
blue and downcast at the burdens of pregnancy: the weight gain, the
clumsiness, the discomforts of many kinds. But I always brushed these
annoyances aside. Through a miracle, an entirely new person was
coming to be, flesh of my flesh. The event was an infusion of grace. At
Christmas—and other days—I remember this privileged time.

And if my own experience was so amazing, it is nothing beside Mary's
exalted experience of grace, in which God took flesh and became one of
us, first as a child in the womb, then as a newborn in the manger. This,
again, is the central mystery of Christmas. It is good that the Church
gives us twelve whole days to contemplate this wonder!

Green, *The Stoning of Saint Stephen.*

The mystery deepens when we reflect on the many appointed feasts during the Christmas cycle. Why have certain feasts been placed in the twelve days between Christmas and the Epiphany? Each day of this Christmas cycle is rich with meaning; each unfolds a story. Often these feasts show us the tension between good and evil, life and death.

134

Emilie Griffin

On this day, December 26, we are looking at that remarkable Christian, the deacon Stephen: the victim of persecution, he was the first to lay down his life for his belief in Jesus Christ.

December 25 is past, but in Stephen's feast our sense of the Incarnation deepens. Stephen said not a word about the infant in the manger. Instead, Stephen's faith was about the full sweep of who Jesus is. Christmas is about wonder, about the mystery of God entering our world; but it is also about how the Incarnation transforms our world, so that even suffering and death can be endured with hope. When Stephen was stoned for his faith and died lifting his eyes to heaven, he showed us the depth and breadth of the Incarnation. That is what we celebrate—not Stephen's death but his full trust in God, much like the trust Jesus had shown in the Garden of Gethsemane. So, it makes sense that we celebrate a martyrdom on the first feast after Christmas Day. God willing, Stephen's faithful witness will continue to show us how to look evil in the face, and how to look through the veil and see our own resurrection with God, as it were, on the other side.

prayer

Dear God, help me to trust in the power of your Incarnate Word even when I do not see the way. Let me not second-guess you. Let me not put my wisdom above yours. Let me believe, Lord, that evil is overcome by your grace. And show me how to forgive my enemies, as Jesus and Stephen did. Teach me to trust in the Incarnation of Christ Jesus, who comes to transform our fallen world. Amen.

history of the feast
December 27

TODAY WE CELEBRATE the feast of Saint John the Evangelist. John was one of the twelve disciples, the younger brother of James. In the Gospels he is referred to as the disciple whom Jesus loved. Though there has been scholarly dispute about whether this John, the author of the Gospel bearing his name, was also the author of the book of Revelation, the ancient church considered them one and the same.

There can be little dispute, however, that both of these New Testament books can help to deepen our understanding of the Incarnation during the Christmas season.

After Jesus' death and resurrection, John preached the gospel for many years, earning the title of "evangelist." The Gospel of John opens with a soaring theological prologue reflecting on the *Logos*, or the "Word": "In the beginning was the Word, and the Word was with God, and the Word was God." As the Word of God, Jesus transcends the world and exists eternally in communion with the Father. But then, John writes, "The Word became flesh and made his dwelling among us." The Greek word he uses for "flesh" is a startlingly earthy, almost crude term for the physical body that Christ adopted in order to become one of us.

As this passage makes clear, John may have been familiar with some of the grander theological and philosophical concepts of his time. But his understanding of the Incarnation makes him steadfastly refuse to turn it into an abstract idea.

Today's reading from John's first letter speaks of the "Word of life" that became flesh. "That which was from the beginning," he says, is also that which "we have seen with our eyes, which we have looked at and our hands have touched."

John was the only disciple who is known not to have been martyred. According to tradition, he served as bishop of Ephesus in Asia Minor and lived to be almost 100. John continued to write into his old age, developing the theme of the Incarnation and looking forward to Christ's final coming, his second advent.

Exiled to the island of Patmos as an old man, he received visions of the end times and recorded them in the Book of Revelation. In this last book of the New Testament we read of the Lord's second coming at the end of time, when history will be fulfilled and all things will be subjected to Christ. This is the second coming that is alluded to throughout the season of Advent.

In the writings of Saint John, we see the link between both kinds of comings: the humble birth of Christ as a helpless babe and his glorious second coming, in which the "body" of his followers will be gathered into the New Jerusalem.

Scripture: *1 John 1:1–4; John 20:2–8*

*Emilie
Griffin*

WHY IS JOHN—the disciple Jesus loved—so important to the Christmas season? I think it is because John, in his friendship with Jesus, showed us how completely God is with us.

There was something quite tangible about the friendship between John and Jesus. John spoke of "what we have heard, what we have seen with our eyes, what we have looked at and touched with our hands, concerning the Word of life." He was describing what it was like to have Jesus as a friend. Their friendship was expressed in concrete ways: walking together, sharing a meal, being in conversation. Can't you just see them kicking up a cloud of dust as they walked along the stony roads around Nazareth, hiking from town to town, talking mostly about the love of God?

But of course this friendship between John and Jesus was also spiritual. This friendship came to life in community. There was nothing exclusive about it, because Jesus was a friend to each of the disciples (just as he is to each of us). The physical things John spoke about, "what we have seen with our own eyes . . . touched with our hands"—all these are outward signs of the spirit that gives life.

Each year when I celebrate Christmas, I notice how concrete it is—all the physical things we do, such as wrapping presents, hanging decorations, sending greeting cards, singing carols, serving good food— these gestures are meant to show peace and goodwill, the *shalom* that exists among good friends. Sometimes these gestures fall short; they fail to reflect the deep inner reality as they should. But (as is so often said about gift-giving) it is the thought that counts: the inner world of soul and spirit is what we mean to express.

El Greco, *Saint John Evangelist.*

Burnand, *Apostles Peter and John Hurry to the Tomb on the Morning of the Resurrection.*

I cherish the yearly flood of Christmas cards as signs of genuine relationships, often with friends who live far away. As the cards arrive, from England, Ireland, Oregon, Minnesota, New York, they express the Incarnation in pictures and words: the stable scene, the wise men on their camels. Even a Christmas stamp may represent a Madonna and Child. It is easy to dismiss Christmas cards as a mandatory social convention. But I treasure this well-worn custom: the family photographs, the folded enclosures, the scribbled messages: "I think of you so often . . . do write and let me hear how you're doing. . . ." Such artless, awkward expressions reflect warm human fellowship. On another level, they are intimations of God dwelling with us.

139

Emilie Griffin

John the beloved disciple tells us about the presence of Jesus. He lived in that presence, both materially and spiritually, day by day, even when he found the empty tomb. When Mary Magdalene saw the stone rolled away, she rushed to find Simon Peter and (as John modestly described himself) the other disciple whom Jesus loved. John ran ahead of Peter, rushed into the empty tomb, went in, and believed. So, today's feast is about the presence of God in Christ, and his bodily resurrection. Jesus is here. Young, affectionate John is also here on this day we set aside for him. He comes to tell us how Jesus loves his friends, so deeply that he gives them his life.

Lord Jesus, I want to feel your presence in my life. Teach me to set aside agendas and objectives so that I may spend time extravagantly with you. Let me seek the peace of going nowhere in particular, doing nothing in particular, but resting in your love. And may I know also the love that is reflected in concrete ways, in fellowship and community. On this feast of your beloved disciple, help me to put love at the center of everything. Amen.

prayer

history of the feast

December 28

THE GOSPEL OF MATTHEW recounts King Herod's reaction to the news of the Incarnation. Herod was the leader of the Jewish people under the authority of Rome during the time of Christ's birth. Cherishing his crown more than anything, he was threatened by the news brought to him by the Magi: that an infant born in Bethlehem would be a king, as the prophets had foretold. In order to eliminate this potential threat to his throne, Herod ordered that all male children in Bethlehem and its vicinity who were two years old and under be killed.

In Christian tradition, the infants murdered at Herod's command have come to be known as the Holy Innocents, or in the East as the Holy Children. The church regards them as martyrs because they died in Christ's place, even though they had no choice. Beginning some time in the fifth century, the church set aside this day to commemorate the martyred children. The liturgical custom is to omit the Gloria and the Alleluia prayers; the clergy once again wear purple instead of the festive colors of Christmas.

As with the celebration of Stephen's martyrdom on December 26, this day reminds us of the inescapable tension between good and evil in a fallen world.

Today, the feast of the Holy Innocents has become a day to honor all young children. In England, this memorial is called Childermas, or Children's Mass. Children are given a blessing; they sing in the choir and take on other special roles in the church service.

Herod was moved to violence out of fear. He failed to see the Incarnation's saving power for all humankind, even for him. Of course, the extreme nature of Herod's action makes any simple comparison with our own lives difficult, and yet at some level we must grapple with the meaning of this event. In our weakness and fragility we are tempted to believe that we can be in control of our lives. But Christ disrupts our lives by coming into the world, challenging our sense of self-reliance. Can any of us say that there isn't a faint shadow of Herod within us, fearful of this threat to our ego?

The Gospel of John puts it this way: "Light has come into the world, but men loved darkness instead of light because their deeds were evil." On this day we should be careful not only to condemn Herod's cruelty, but also our own blindness to the significance of the Incarnation.

Nolde, *Christ among the Children.*

Scripture: *1 John 1:5–2:2; Matthew 2:13–18*

*Emilie
Griffin*

Tᴏᴅᴀʏ'ѕ ꜰᴇᴀѕᴛ ᴏᴘᴇɴѕ ᴜᴘ ᴀɴᴏᴛʜᴇʀ ᴡᴀʏ ᴛᴏ ʟᴏᴏᴋ ᴀᴛ ᴛʜᴇ Iɴᴄᴀʀɴᴀᴛɪᴏɴ. Until now we have been gazing at the child in the cradle, the scene of the Nativity, the angels rejoicing. But Herod's story was one of rage, jealousy, and fear.

Herod the Great, despite his high office as the Tetrarch of Galilee, was afraid of the long-promised Messiah. When he heard from the Magi that such a royal heir had been born right within his jurisdiction, he was alarmed and resorted immediately to subterfuge. Wouldn't the Magi please let him know where he could find this child and worship him? Then, when the Magi foiled his plan, Herod employed a familiar tactic: violence. The slaughter of the innocents, so often depicted in great Renaissance paintings, is a grisly tale. How does this story of murder and bloodshed bring us closer to the Prince of Peace?

Herod personified all the ways that dictatorial power can oppress us. When I look around the contemporary world, I see that many are still cast in Herod's mold: power-crazy, filled with rage, fearfully insecure. They're threatened by the possibility that someone will overthrow them, and they'll go to any lengths to destroy their rivals. But God is not on the side of the oppressor. Divine favor rests instead on the holy child at Bethlehem. God himself came into our world as a child. Do we really believe the words of Mary's prayer? *He has brought down the powerful from their thrones, and lifted up the lowly.*

This ancient story reminds me of power struggles we face in contemporary life: not just among nations and organizations but in our personal lives. I think of contentious board meetings, cranky committee discussions, office politics, churches filled with dissension. Antagonism

Poussin, *Massacre of the Innocents.*

seems to crop up everywhere. As much as in Herod's time, we need the Prince of Peace.

How is it that the power of the Incarnate Lord begins to work in hostile situations? I think it is not when we point our fingers at modern Herods but when we look within ourselves, wanting to live as Jesus did. Are we people of forgiveness and goodwill? Am I on Herod's side, or on the side of the innocents? When something or someone gets in my way, do I strike out, using imperious commands? Do I seek power for myself more often than reconciliation with others ?

Unless we are really attentive, we might miss the Incarnate power expressed in this brief, sacred story, with its mythical quality that makes it seem like a fairy tale. Many guiltless children died so that Jesus could live. God's tremendous power entered our world in the form of a defenseless child, and the story of whether peace or violence will win in our lives is still being played out each day.

prayer

Lord, give me hope. Let me see your providential hand at work in every corner of society. And let me be refreshed by the innocence of children, Lord. Let me be amused by their antics, their sudden laughter, their glee. Help me to be touched by the naiveté of the Christmas narrative, the angels bringing word to humanity, Mary and Joseph escaping with their child into Egypt. May the light of the Incarnation flood my heart. Help me bring your peace into the world. Amen.

December 29

Scripture: *1 John 2:3–11; Luke 2:22–35*

Emilie Griffin

ON THIS DAY WE REMEMBER SIMEON, one of the most important witnesses to the Incarnation. Little is known about Simeon except what the Gospel tells us: "This man was righteous and devout, looking forward to the consolation of Israel, and the Holy Spirit rested on him."[2] Also, he was there in the Temple at Jerusalem when Joseph and Mary took their young child to present him to the Lord.

The Holy Spirit had made Simeon an extraordinary promise. Simeon would live to lay eyes on the Lord's Messiah.

The Spirit guided Simeon into the Temple just when Joseph and Mary were arriving. Simeon took the child into his arms and praised God. "Master, now you are dismissing your servant in peace," begins Simeon's brief but beautiful song, or canticle, long known by its Latin name, *Nunc Dimittis*. His heart overflowed because God had allowed him to see this manifestation of God. This too is a "showing," an epiphany (the word means "manifestation" or "showing").

I'm reminded of that phrase by C.S. Lewis: "the tether and pang of the particular." I can remember moments in my own life when a very ordinary activity brought me a profound sense of blessing. And if I had known the words of the *Nunc Dimittis* by heart, I certainly would have sung them!

Simeon's sense of God's fulfilled promise makes the scene in the Temple profound. Nothing could have been more ordinary for a Jewish couple than to take their newborn son to the Temple to be dedicated to God. They bought a pair of turtledoves in accordance with Jewish law, as a sacrifice for God's graciousness. Mary and Joseph were practicing

Rembrandt, *Simeon and Hannah in the Temple.*

their religion in a most ordinary way. But the whole experience is shot through with joy, as well as a hint of the sorrow to come.

We may never lose sight of the mystery of Christ, even in these ordinary events. The Gospel returns us to mystery again and again. Who can forget Simeon's words to Mary: "And a sword will pierce your own soul, too." In this one sentence Simeon foresees a consequence of the Incarnation that perhaps even the child's mother had not yet understood.

In our own lives we will also have glimpses of God's love, small epiphanies, our own moments to sing our *Nunc Dimittis*. These glimpses are given to us, I think, when we are faithful to his word.

prayer

Dear God, my life is a maze of ordinary things: work, family, church, correspondence, bill-paying, filling out forms. Help me to see that in fulfilling my obligations I am serving you. Let me be open to the grace of the random encounter. Give me glimpses of your reality in the middle of things. Let me recognize the Messiah, as Simeon did. And help me to live by your commandment of love, no matter what the cost. Amen.

146

Emilie Griffin

Rembrandt, *Simeon and Hannah in the Temple.*

Tanner, *The Thankful Poor.*

December 30

Scripture: *1 John 2:12–17; Luke 2:36–40*

Emilie Griffin

FOR MANY OF US CHRISTMAS IS A TIME OF PLENTY: lavish meals, parties, giving gifts and receiving them, taking them back for exchange, assembling children's toys on living room carpets, hunting for the right size batteries when not provided. By the sixth day of Christmas, if not sooner, this overabundance has worn us out.

But the Incarnation overturns this way of thinking. John in his first letter cautions us against worldliness, which he calls the "desire of the flesh, the desire of the eyes." This is good advice for those who are overwhelmed by the retail aspects of the holiday. Christ, plunged into history, must be the guiding force of all our loves, hopes, and desires.

Anna, the woman we meet today in Luke's Gospel, has it right. This eighty-four-year-old woman, the daughter of Phanuel of the tribe of Asher, "never left the temple but worshiped there with fasting and prayer night and day." Does she remind you of some older folks you know, who love to be in church much of the time? Anna was called a prophet. No doubt her intense prayer life had opened her up to a deeper vision. She recognized the Christ-child and his meaning for "all who were looking for the redemption of Jerusalem." Are we, too, looking for the redemption of Jerusalem? And do we have eyes to recognize the Christ-child?

The Incarnation gives meaning to our celebration, turning our feast into more than the desire of the flesh or of the eyes. Christmas is about a godly yearning, a desire for the Love that will make us whole and complete. If we are enlightened and wise, we do not give or receive gifts except for the sake of that greater love, a godly love that transforms everything.

Lotto, *The Presentation in the Temple.*

To use a popular phrase, Jesus is the reason for the season. The child who returned to Nazareth in Galilee, who matured there, who grew in the grace and favor of the Father, is the one whose generous love can inspire all our giving, all our receiving. In him the world of matter and spirit are joined, and created things are shot through with meaning. In the words of Gerard Manley Hopkins, "the world is charged with the grandeur of God." This God-charged world is never a world of pride in riches or desire of the eyes; no, it is the redeemed world of God's desiring.

150

Emilie Griffin

prayer

Dear Christ, teach me to love your world and everyone in it. May I love with an unworldly love. Let me understand the godly use of material things, to delight rightly in your creation. May I remember those words from John's first letter: "those who do the will of God live forever." Amen.

New Year's Eve
December 31

Scripture: *1 John 2:18–21; John 1:1–18*

Emilie Griffin

THE WORLD OF THE GOSPELS was not too different from ours. Even in our day of airport screenings and frequent arrests, behind barricades of military buildup and international alliances, in spite of all our advanced defense technologies, we know our world is precarious and can collapse as suddenly as the Twin Towers. Our only security is in God: God with us.

John wrote to those in his community to encourage them in an anxious time. He warned them that the day of reckoning was close at hand. "Children, it is the last hour!" This may not sound much like reassurance but it certainly got their attention. John's "children"—those he nourished in faith—were upset about people defecting from the true faith. They felt their world was falling apart, and John meant to reassure them.

Anxiety makes good headlines today. We read that the polar caps are melting, we are running out of fossil fuels, the climate is changing, the animal kingdom is being affected by high technology. These are not delusional statements. They have basis in fact, and they often convince us, along with many other aspects of modern life, that we are living in the last hours or days of planet Earth.

John's words, written centuries ago, have an apocalyptic tone. But his deeper message is meant for childlike hearts. He offers, not words of panic, but of peace and reassurance. We who know Christ, who receive him, who believe in his name, receive power to become children of God. "And the Word became flesh and lived among us, and we have seen his glory, the glory as of a father's only son, full of grace and truth."

de La Tour, *Saint Joseph the Carpenter.*

By living the Christian life on the deepest possible level, we remain secure in God no matter how fearful the times. How do we do this? Not by denying the uncomfortable facts of our environment and our troubled societies, but by letting the Incarnate Christ transform us. The God life within us will strengthen us in times of war and peace. And with transformed hearts we will do what we can for our anxious neighbors and our societies.

To be conscious that we are children of God, we must pay attention. We must practice the Christian life with confident spirits. Keeping the Incarnate Christ close to us, in our hearts, we internalize God's Word. By putting ourselves at the service of Christ, we are transformed. "From his fullness we have all received, grace upon grace." Even if it is the last hour, it is the hour of redemption for those who believe.

152

Emilie Griffin

prayer

Dear Lord, there are signs of trouble and anxiety all around me. Give me confidence to trust in your incarnate presence in a fearful world. Help me know that I am a child of God. Amen.

history of the feast

January 1

O N JANUARY 1, the church celebrates the feast of Mary, the Mother of God, meditating on Mary's intimate connection with the Incarnation. The feast of the Mother of God is the oldest of the Christian church's feasts honoring Mary. The placement of this feast within the Christmas season emphasizes its connection to the mystery of Christmas.

Because this feast is about the motherhood of Mary, it helps us to grasp more deeply the meaning of the Incarnation: God himself born to a human mother. This day celebrates Mary's most important title: the *Theotokos*, or "God-bearer." *Theotokos* is the Greek term from which we derive the name "Mother of God." This title was attributed to Mary from the first centuries of Christendom, and was upheld at the Council of Ephesus in 431.

Rather than limiting Mary's title to *Christotokos*, or "Christ-bearer," the council agreed on the importance of understanding Mary as the mother of God. To call her the mother of Christ but not the mother of God would imply that somehow Christ's humanity is separate from his divinity. The title of God-bearer holds Christ's divinity and his humanity in perfect balance. Thus, in contemplating Mary as "Mother of God," we are contemplating the nature of the Incarnation: God and man, inseparable in the person of Christ.

Mary's role in the Incarnation began when she accepted the astonishing news brought to her by the angel Gabriel: that she would bear the Son of God. Her "Yes" to God is a model of faith and obedience. Despite the terrifying prospects of accepting her calling, she yielded her

very body to the will of God, saying, "I am the Lord's servant. May it be to me as you have said."

The placement of this feast at the beginning of the calendar year reminds us that Jesus' birth ushered in a new era. This day aligns our Christmas celebration with Mary's maternal joy at the birth of her son. Today is also the "octave," or eighth day, of Christmas. According to God's Covenant with the Israelites, male children were circumcised on the eighth day after they were born. So this day also recalls the outward, sacramental sign of Christ's consecration to God, along with Mary's role in the child's life and in the life of the church.

History of the Feast

Scripture: *Numbers 6:22–27;*
Galatians 4:4–7; Luke 2:16–21

155

Emilie
Griffin

BUT MARY TREASURED ALL THESE WORDS and pondered them in her heart." Whenever I hear this Scripture I remember how we used to put on the Nativity Play in our small, all-girls high school. Every year the performance began with comic entertainment reflecting current themes, followed by the Nativity pageant that was invariably the same: the seniors staged and performed the play, acting all the parts. I vividly recall lanky girls dressed up as shepherds, in burlap with sandals. I remember the Magi parading down the aisle in robes and turbans.

Then the music began. The lower school choir sang "The Friendly Beasts" in high, angelic voices. Our hearts melted. A hush descended. Next the Bible story, in the familiar King James Version, was read aloud. Despite amateur rough edges, this was a sacred time. Tension built up in the audience. "Who will play Mary this year?" "It's such an honor." "Can you guess?" She would be the girl we most admired, most worthy, kindest, best.

At last the curtains parted, and there she was in her sea-blue gown, bending over the child in the hay. Joseph (also played by a senior girl) knelt steadfastly beside her. For a moment, the ancient story came to life in front of us. As the play ended we heard these words: "Mary kept all these things and pondered them in her heart."

Mary, Mother of God. Her place in salvation-history calls forth high compliments and lavish phrases. It is easy to be drawn to the life of Mary. I like to see her as a modest young woman living in Nazareth, friendly, fun-loving, sensitive, devout. I can imagine her sewing, mending,

Russian icon, *Mother of God, Eleousa of Vladimir.*

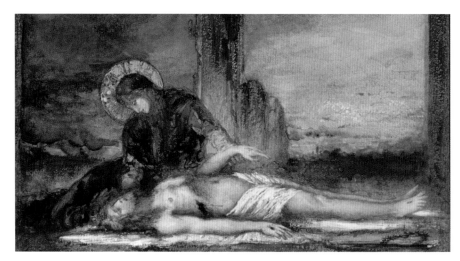

Moreau, *Pietà*.

Emilie Griffin

drawing water, making bread; getting to know Joseph, exchanging vows with him; greeting the angel graciously; visiting with her cousin Elizabeth. Finally, I see her in the stable at Bethlehem, adoring the most wonderful child ever born. I like to reflect on Mary's depth of soul, and on how she pondered amazing things in her heart.

She was not only the one who bore Christ in the flesh. She was also the one who followed Christ, who showed us how to be completely faithful to him. Mary showed us how to contemplate Jesus, even in his last hours of trial. No longer the young girl of Nazareth, this was the Mary whose soul had been pierced by a sword.

prayer

Father in heaven, help me to learn from Mary, who pondered things in her heart. When I most need Jesus, let me look with Mary's way of contemplation: attentive, practical, affectionate.

Like Mary, I want to reflect on the mystery of the Incarnation, on how God became man and lived with us, and on how Christ's continuing presence quickens and transforms us. Amen.

January 2

Scripture: *1 John 2:22–28; John 1:19–28*

Emilie Griffin

I REMEMBER MY OWN BAPTISM VIVIDLY, in a New York church when I was twenty-five years old. This wasn't the moment that I accepted Christ, for I had done that long before. But it was a deeply dramatic moment when all the imagery of baptism—the reality of Christ—came home to me in a new way. You could say it was a kind of an epiphany: a manifestation. God's truth was shown clearly to me, and I was showing my own faith by wanting to "die with Christ."

I like to think that the forms we use, the sacraments and ceremonies, are ways we give ourselves completely to God. Some people want to pray demonstratively. They kneel; they raise their hands; they even lie flat on the ground or on a cold, stone floor, prostrating themselves before God. It is their way of saying, "Lord, I am fully present to you, I am yours entirely." For others, baptism expresses this total gift of self and becomes a spiritual or physical anointing.

"You anoint my head with oil; my cup overflows," says Psalm 23. Throughout the Bible anointing is an entrance into royal status, conferring divine favor. "How good, how delightful it is to live as brothers all together! It is like a fine oil on the head, running down the beard, running down Aaron's beard, onto the collar of his robes." Such ancient, simple signs, clear baptismal water and rich holy oil, have not outlived their usefulness. We long to become God's people, yet we fear our own divided selves, our ambivalence, our reluctance to commit. Therefore we want to place ourselves under the seal of a godly promise.

El Greco, *Saints John the Baptist and John the Evangelist.*

158

*Emilie
Griffin*

del Sarto, *Saint John the Baptist Baptizing.*

Still, spiritual signs are only as good as what they signify: a real conversion of heart. Baptizing is brief. Anointing does not last long. But the promise we make must continue: to pray, fast, serve, confess our sins, study the Scripture, and become more steadfast daily. Real commitment does not fade or evaporate. In Paul's words, "Even though our outer nature is wasting away, our inner nature is being renewed day by day."

prayer

Dear God, help me to value and practice the language of sign and sacrament. Make me attentive to all the signs of your life in us. And continue in me a full conversion of heart, today, and all year. Amen.

January 3

Scripture: *1 John 2:29, 3:1–6; John 1:29–34*

*Emilie
Griffin*

MANY CHRISTIANS HAVE SPOKEN OF PURIFICATION as a necessary stage in the spiritual life, a cleansing that comes by fits and starts, requires patient endurance, and is not always accompanied by flashes of light. Evelyn Underhill speaks of this purgative way as "a dreadful joy" and "an earnest of increasing life." John of the Cross describes the dark night of the senses and the dark night of the soul. This dark night is part of our progress toward God. As we come closer to the light, we are temporarily blinded by the divine power. In such circumstances we need the assurance John the Evangelist gives: "See what love the Father has given us." On days when we feel somewhat less than sanctified, we need to remember John's promise: "Beloved, we are God's children now." Christ's love and the Father's love are changing us, making us pure, whether or not we fully grasp this love.

Is this purification happening? How, exactly? It is not only in prayer that Jesus changes us. Purification may come about through the sometimes consoling, sometimes buffeting effects of our personal relationships. Suppose that a man challenges you at a community meeting. "You haven't done your homework," he tells you. "Your presumptions are foolish and false." He makes you angry, and you want to dismiss his challenges as useless ideas. But you sense that some truth is speaking to you through this person's anxiety and anger. Something within you says, "See the Christ in him. Jesus may be speaking to me here." This difficult committee member is like the street beggar to whom you must give a cup of cold water in Christ's name. *Be even-handed with him,* the Lord whispers. *Listen to what he has to say. You are a child of God, but so is he.* Often this is how Jesus speaks, through some

Zurbaran, *Agnus Dei.*

inner prompting, some influence of grace. His generous love teaches us how to act in difficult situations, when people try our patience.

We don't usually meet Jesus in the Galilean countryside, or on the banks of the Jordan River, as John the Baptist did, but rather, through an inward encounter with the help of the Holy Spirit. Even so, Christ is changing us; and when we are attentive, we know it. He is purifying us with his love. Today's readings converge to tell us how, through the Son, our transformation is happening. "See what love the Father has given us, that we should be called children of God; and that is what we are."

It isn't only in moments of difficulty that Christ is forming us. Our friends also help us to change, to become better, to relax, to be faithful. We learn to practice self-control, self-restraint, seeking virtue, avoiding sin. In these ways Christ comes to live in us. "What we do know is this: when he is revealed, we will be like him; for we will see him as he is." Doesn't this make perfect sense? Our divine Friend, Jesus—because of the Incarnation—makes God's power available to us in purifying ways.

160

Emilie Griffin

prayer

Dear God, help me to know that I am your child. Teach me to weigh the meaning of this title "Children of God." Show me the power of your purifying love, and make me patient for my own transformation. Amen.

Scripture: *1 John 3:7–10; John 1:35–42*

Emilie
Griffin

THE DAY AFTER JESUS WAS BAPTIZED BY JOHN, after the Holy Spirit had descended on him, there's a short account of two disciples following after Jesus. These two had heard John the Baptizer pointing Jesus out as the Lamb of God. They trailed after him until Jesus turned and confronted them. He wanted to know what they were up to. "Rabbi," they said to him, "where are you staying?"

I love the homeliness of this account. What simple questions! "Where are you going? Where are you staying?" But best of all, Jesus invited the men to spend the afternoon with him. "They came and saw where he was staying, and they remained with him that day."

Friendship begins like that: spending time together, even wasting time together, exploring the great issues of life and death, but in a haphazard, leisurely way. Like an afternoon when one's philosophy class is being held on the lawn, as though one had all the time in the world. It reminds me of a line of Annie Dillard's: "Spend the afternoon. You can't take it with you."

Throughout the New Testament we notice this sort of homeliness surrounding the Incarnation. In Jesus, God is completely present to the rest of us. Young men gather around him. A woman wants to touch the hem of his garment and be healed. And Jesus wants them to come. He says, "Come and see." Being close to Jesus, experiencing intimate friendship with him—that's the seed of our transformation. That's why the Father sent the Son to us: to cross the unbridgeable distance, to show us splendor in the ordinary, to be *that close*.

Santvoort, *The Supper at Emmaus.*

162

*Emilie
Griffin*

Leonardo da Vinci, *Saint Anne with Virgin and Child Playing with the Lamb.*

Even before a word is on my tongue,
O LORD, you know it completely.
You hem me in, behind and before,
and lay your hand upon me. [13]

PRAYER   *Dear Lord, make yourself known to me, as you did to your followers, in the middle of ordinary life. I want to believe I can be changed through closeness to you, and to the community surrounding me. Protect me from sin and evil by the power of your grace. Amen.*

January 5

Scripture: *1 John 3:11–21; John 1:43–51*

Emilie Griffin

THE CHRISTMAS SEASON IS DRAWING TO A CLOSE. But in the two remaining days there is a chance to tap into a deep understanding of what the Incarnation means.

In today's Gospel we see an inexperienced community of disciples beginning to form. First there were two, the ones who lingered with Jesus until four in the afternoon. Andrew and his companion were amazed that they had found the Messiah. They brought Simon in on the secret, and Jesus gave him a nickname, "The Rock." The next day Jesus found Philip, and said to him, "Follow me." Philip then brought in Nathaniel. One by one the community of disciples took shape. Were they pulled together by a common dream for a better future? Possibly. But perhaps they also simply enjoyed spending time with Jesus and each other. "Can anything good come out of Nazareth?" they joked, referring to the ministry of Jesus. They didn't take themselves too seriously. Still, they sensed that God was in their midst.

Community is one of the ways that Jesus becomes present to me. When faith is the unifier, the groups I belong to allow me to know Jesus better, to spend time with him just as the first disciples did. We discuss what we care about and yearn for. Our common longing for insight helps us to open our hearts to each other.

One group I belong to spent half a year reading *The Four Loves* by C.S. Lewis. Perhaps the tenderest moment for me came when we talked about the sometimes instantaneous way that friendships form between women. Such a bond can be just like love at first sight! We were a bit embarrassed, but we had to admit it was true. Memories

Vinckeboons, *Peasant Kermesse (Country Party)*.

stirred. Suddenly I saw before me the face of Catherine Williams, my lifelong friend who died in 1997. How quickly our friendship had first sprung to life, when we worked together in Manhattan, in the corridors of a New York City skyscraper! How thoroughly we had shared the joys of marriage, childbearing, teenage children, baptisms, birthdays, anniversaries. Even when Catherine had moved to London, in spite of distance, the friendship had continued strong. To me, it was God-given. And as Lewis says, the friendship was nonexclusive. It was about not only "us two" but also a whole circle of friends, all of us warmly united.

Love is about showing, about manifestation, about epiphany. I could hardly describe, even in this one instance, the innumerable small demonstrative gestures of that friendship: lending a christening gown, making transatlantic phone calls on birthdays, exchanging photos and photo albums, getting together for children's birthdays and wedding anniversaries. Love is demonstrable. It is expressed in visible ways. "For this is the message you have heard from the beginning, that we should love one another." And if there are such gestures defining one friendship, think how in a larger circle they may multiply, until the whole community of disciples abides in love.

164

*Emilie
Griffin*

prayer

Father in Heaven, thank you for the deep friendships you have given me, and for the wisdom to appreciate them. Thank you also for the presence of your Son. Amen.

history of the feast

January 6

THE FEAST OF EPIPHANY is the final feast day of the Christmas season. It celebrates those events in Christ's early life that revealed his divine nature to those around him. In a larger sense, this feast reminds us that the Incarnation involves the announcement of salvation to "all nations." The Good News is not for a privileged group but for everyone everywhere.

Epiphany comes from the Greek word *epiphaneia*, which is translated both as "coming" and as "manifestation" or "appearing." While Christmas celebrates Christ's *coming* in the Incarnation event, Epiphany celebrates *manifestation*—the ways in which the Incarnation is revealed to us.

The feast of Epiphany originated in the Eastern Church. It was celebrated as early as the third century, even before Christmas was part of the liturgical calendar. For early Christians, Epiphany was primarily a feast celebrating the manifestation of Christ at his baptism, when it was revealed to those present that Jesus was the Messiah and the Son of God. The feast also celebrated other events that revealed Christ's identity to the world, including the Magi's adoration of the Christ-child and Jesus' first miracle at the wedding at Cana.

In the early church, Epiphany was also a commemoration of Christ's nativity—God made manifest through his literal appearance in the flesh. This changed in the fourth century, when the church began to observe the feast of the Incarnation on Christmas Day. As December 25 became the sole feast devoted to Christ's nativity, the focus of Epiphany was narrowed to commemorate other important manifestations of Christ.

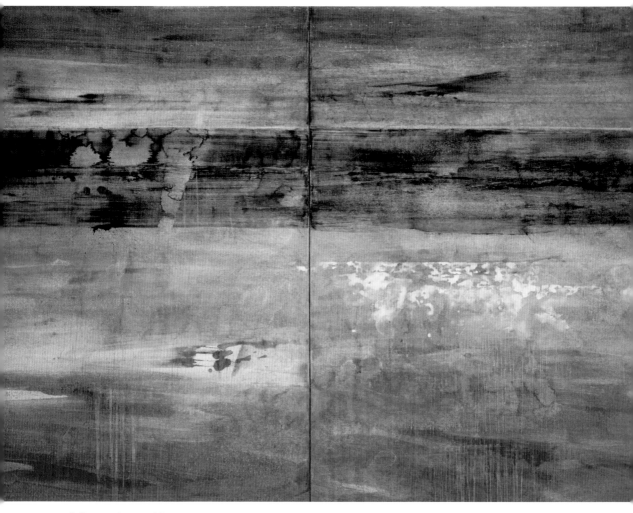

Fujimura, *January Hour.*

Scripture: *Isaiah 60:1–6;*
Ephesians 3:2–3a, 5–6; Matthew 2:1–12

Emilie
Griffin

IN MANY CHRISTIAN LANDS Epiphany is the most important feast of Christmas. Especially in Latin countries the arrival of the Wise Men, the Three Kings, looms large in the imagination. My native city, New Orleans, is heir to a European, especially French and Spanish, heritage. Twelfth Night not only concludes the Christmas season, but also inaugurates the festive days of Carnival, leading up to Shrove Tuesday or Mardi Gras. King cakes, into which small trinkets or favors are baked, express the joyfulness of this date in the Christian calendar. Bakeries offer these festive cakes in New Orleans and throughout Louisiana. In Shakespeare's England, Twelfth Night was such a big day that special entertainments were composed just for that occasion. In Latin countries, Epiphany is the biggest day of the whole Christmas season, when gifts are exchanged to recall the gifts of the Magi.

But for most of us English speakers, this feast (which is sometimes observed on the nearest Sunday) might slip by. Epiphany is rarely a large-scale festival, and it seems that our religious imagination may have let us down. The Christmas season is ending. Christmas trees have been removed, their cast-off needles swept away. Possibly, among traditionalists, a small crèche still occupies a place of honor in the parlor. On the church lawn or a side altar, the Christmas scene remains. Finally the Magi have arrived, bringing gold, frankincense, and myrrh.

> Nations shall come to your light,
> and kings to the brightness of your dawn. . . .
> They shall bring gold and frankincense,
> and shall proclaim the praise of the LORD.

Bosch, *The Adoration of the Magi.*

I sometimes feel that what moderns need most is renewal of the religious imagination. We need big mental pictures of kings who parade before us on their camels; they should be large, exaggerated, gorgeous figures in *papier-mâché*. Because, as Paul explains to the Ephesians, a new mystery has been revealed: "In former generations this mystery was not made known to humankind . . . that is, the Gentiles have become fellow heirs, members of the same body, and sharers in the promise in Christ Jesus through the gospel."

Most of all, we need to imagine, to conceive of the sovereignty of God.

In ancient times many people guided their lives by the stars and constellations. The zodiac provided a frame of reference for divinity. And the lives of great men were usually ushered in and out by comets: "When beggars die, there are no comets seen," Shakespeare wrote. "The heavens themselves blaze forth the death of princes." In Matthew's account of the Magi, the astrologers were following a star that eventually stopped over the place where the young child lay.

The twelfth day of Christmas—the Epiphany—is about God making this sovereignty known not just to Israel but also to all the peoples of the world. To understand this story, we need imagination: the eyes not of rationalism but of revelation. The Christmas season begins with incarnation and ends with manifestation. The star that guided the Magi was governed, not by gases and gravity, but by God's desire to convey a message to his people. It is a majestic story meant to be embroidered in tapestries shot through with gold.

prayer

Dear Lord, give me a new depth of vision to understand the mysteries of your revelation. Let me grasp the full revolution brought about by your reign. Let me absorb the wisdom of your ancient story, which sets aside the domination of kings like Herod and ushers in kings who worship, who surrender, who are awed by the dimensions of divine power.

Give me, also, Lord, a spirit of celebration, so I can revel in the magnitude of your joy and your renewal of the human heart. Amen.

history of the feast

THE FEAST OF THE HOLY FAMILY upholds the family of Jesus, Mary, and Joseph as a model for Christian families everywhere. The celebration of this feast is relatively new, first appearing in the liturgy at the end of the nineteenth century and officially adopted into the Roman church calendar in 1921. Observed on the first Sunday after Christmas, this holy day reminds us of the important role that family played in Jesus' life, and of its importance in the life of the church.

Celebrated within a week of the feast of the Incarnation, the Holy Family emphasizes Jesus' humanity: God chose to become present to us by being born into an ordinary human family. The experience of family is integral to being human, and the fact that Christ's Incarnation took place within a family emphasizes Christ's humanity. In his Incarnation, Jesus not only adopted a human body but also became familiar with the very ordinary challenges and struggles of family life. He truly became one of us.

In addition to revealing Christ's humanity, this feast reminds the faithful of the important role that family plays in the Christian life. Living in a family as God intended has the potential to make us more Christlike. We look to Mary and Joseph, and to their relationship with their son, as a model of the mutual love, respect, and trust essential to the Christian family.

The Gospel readings in the liturgy for this feast day cycle among three important events in the early life of Jesus' family: the flight into Egypt, the presentation of Jesus in the temple, and Mary and Joseph's discovery of Jesus in the temple. Each of these events demonstrates the involvement of Mary and Joseph in their son's calling. Their acts of faith and obedience to God are a model of parental care: protecting, nurturing, and ultimately letting go.

It is customary for families to say a special prayer of blessing for their children on this day, and for couples to renew their marriage vows. We bring the holy family to mind during the week after Christmas in order to reflect more deeply on the meaning of Christ's humanity. Because Jesus became one of us, there is no aspect of humanity with which he is unfamiliar—including both the struggles and the blessings experienced within the context of family life. While our human families will always fall short of the ideal, we can find comfort and encouragement in the faith, hope, and love that are exemplified in the holy family of Nazareth.

Scripture: *Psalm 127; Colossians 3:12–21;*
Luke 2:22–40

171

Emilie
Griffin

THE HOLY FAMILY is often held up to us as a model for conduct. Jesus, Mary and Joseph are the romantic ideal of family life. But sometimes we may find it hard to accept them as examples, because we suppose they are specially privileged in ways to which we can't aspire. Jesus is sinless; Mary is spotless; Joseph is kindly, loyal, protective; and they're all descended from a royal line.

Sometimes, when I think of the Holy Family, I remember the carved wooden crèche we had when our children were small. Even though the crèche was expensive, we let the children play with the figures. Soon the sheep had lost one leg. The haloes on Joseph and Mary were twisted. The manger scene was a bit out of whack.

That helps me to remember that Joseph, Mary, and Jesus were all tested in virtue. And they lived, as we do, in a broken world.

It's rare to think of the Holy Family of Joseph, Mary, and Jesus as resembling the families we live in. Because they are set before us as ideals of perfection, we think they had no problems at all. But authentic virtue is all about struggle. Everything isn't done for us. I remember once, when our children were small, my husband and I had an argument during Christmas, overheard by one of our daughters who stood nearby playing with the crèche. Instead of addressing herself to us, she acted out the quarrel with the figures in the crèche, speaking in and through them. "Don't cry, Joseph and Mary," she said. "Everything will be all right." She had grasped the humanity of the Holy Family fairly well.

Annigoni, *Saint Joseph.*

If Jesus and Mary are models to us of what virtuous living should be, we should imagine them caught in the web of family tensions, exerting themselves to be good—just as we are caught in similar struggles—but empowered by God's presence and love.

Today's reading from St. Paul's letter to the Colossians makes good sense. First the Colossians are addressed as "God's chosen ones, holy and beloved." But then they're told to get a new wardrobe: "Clothe yourselves with compassion, kindness, humility, meekness, and patience." These virtues are more than superficial adornments. "If anyone has a complaint against another, forgive each other; just as the Lord has forgiven you, so you must also forgive." We must follow the way of love, doing everything in the name of Christ. This sort of clothing is not for show; it's a kind of inner garment, visible by the choices we make and the forgiveness we offer.

This kind of goodness is most severely tested at the places where we spend most of our time: at work in, church, in community gatherings, at school board meetings. But most often, our charity begins (or doesn't begin) at home. The family is the proving ground of virtue. Spiritual friendship provides us with a clue. Our closest spiritual friends are rarely the ones we're closely related to. And why would that be? There's homework still to be done.

We need to claim the idea of "holy family" for ourselves. Mary, Joseph, and Jesus had their problems and we have ours. We need to grasp their humanity until they are not just plaster saints, but living models of holiness in a broken world.

172

Emilie
Griffin

prayer

Dear God, let the Incarnate Word dwell in me richly and teach me to forgive. God, give me the grace to thank you for my family, and for the Holy Family. Amen.

Crespi, *Holy Family.*

da Messina, *Crucifixion.*

notes

175

Introduction

p. 4   *the Word became flesh . . . among us*   John 1:14 (RSV)

p. 4   *first-born of all creation*   Colossians 1:15 (RSV). Jesus is also designated "first-born" in other contexts: "first-born among many brethren," Romans 8:29; "first-born from the dead," Colossians 1:18 and Revelation 1:5; and "first-born into the world," Hebrews 1:6 (RSV).

p. 5   *We have established . . . secret of creation*   Karl Barth, *Church Dogmatics* (Edinburgh: T & T Clark, ET 1958), Vol. III, Part 1, 28. Reprinted by permission of The Continuum International Publishing Group.

p. 5   *This is God's initiative . . . has dreamed of*   Raymond Brown, *The Birth of the Messiah* (Garden City, NY: Doubleday & Co., Inc., 1977), 314. Used by permission of the Associates Sulpicians of the U.S.

p. 5   *born of woman*   Galatians 4:4 (RSV)

p. 5   *in the last resort . . . all too far-off God*   Karl Barth, *Credo* (NY: Charles Scribner's Sons, 1962), 68.

p. 6   *This is the irrational . . . for the child*   Madeleine L'Engle. Reprinted from *The Weather of the Heart.* Copyright © 1978, 2001 by Crosswicks, Ltd. Used by permission of WaterBrook Press, Colorado Springs, CO. All rights reserved.

p. 6   *born anew*   John 3:7 (RSV)

p. 6   *as if in the pangs of childbirth*   Romans 8:22 (REB)

p. 6   *identified himself to the Galatians*   Galatians 4:19 (NRSV)

First Week of Advent

p. 19   *It is full time . . . wake from sleep*   Romans 13:11 (RSV)

p. 19   *Let it be to me according to your word*   Luke 1:38 (RSV)

p. 21   *I will come . . . found such faith*   Matthew 8:5–10 (RSV)

p. 25   *A little child shall lead them*   Isaiah 11:6 (RSV)

p. 25   *Glory to God . . . he is pleased*   Luke 2:14 (RSV)

p. 25   *Woe to those . . . there is no peace*   Jeremiah 6:14 (Author's rendering)

p. 25   *Peace I leave . . . neither let them be afraid*   John 14:27 (RSV)

p. 26   *Fear not . . . the kingdom*   Luke 12:32 (RSV)

p. 27   *With God all things are possible*   Matthew 19:26 (RSV)

p. 28   *In the beginning . . . has not overcome it*   John 1:1, 3–5 (RSV)

p. 31   *Therefore . . . about your life*   Matthew 6:25 (RSV)

p. 31   *Hail, O favored one . . . greeting this might be*   Luke 1:28–29 (RSV)

p. 31   *Behold . . . according to your word*   Luke 1:38 (RSV)

p. 32   *Not my will but yours be done*   Luke 22:42b (NRSV)

p. 32   *Our Father . . . as it is in heaven*   Matthew 6:9, 10 (NRSV)

p. 33   *in that day*   Isaiah 29:18 (RSV)

p. 33   *Do you believe . . . eyes were opened*   Matthew 9:28–30 (RSV)

p. 38   *harassed and helpless . . . laborers into the harvest*   Matthew 9:36b, 38 (RSV)

p. 38   *Lo . . . close of the age*   Matthew 28:20 (RSV)

p. 38   *He who hears you . . . him who sent me*   Luke 10:16 (RSV)

p. 42   *Well done, good and faithful servant*   Matthew 25:21, 23 (RSV)

p. 42   *I came . . . have it abundantly*   John 10:10b (RSV)

Second Week of Advent

p. 51   *The wilderness . . . joy and singing*   Isaiah 35:1–2a (RSV)

p. 54   *If a man . . . little ones should perish*   Matthew 18:12, 13–14 (RSV)

p. 54   *All we like sheep . . . opened not his mouth*   Isaiah 53:6–7 (RSV)

p. 57   *To whom then . . . says the Holy One*   Isaiah 40:25 (RSV)

p. 57   *Lift up your eyes . . . all by name*   Isaiah 40:26a (RSV)

p. 58   *He gives power . . . and not faint*   Isaiah 40:29–31 (RSV)

p. 58   *Come to me . . . burden is light*   Matthew 11:28–30 (RSV)

p. 59   *see and know . . . has created it*   Isaiah 41:20 (RSV)

p. 63   *I am the LORD . . . destroyed from before me*   Isaiah 48:17b–19 (RSV)

p. 71   *one who hears the word of God and does it*   Cf. Matthew 13:23

Third Week of Advent

p. 78   *Waiting does not diminish . . . joyful our expectancy*   Romans 8:24–25 (THE MESSAGE)

p. 78   *let endurance . . . mature and complete*   James 1:4 (NRSV)

p. 78   *I wait . . . in his word I hope*   Psalm 130:5 (NRSV)

Notes

p. 79 *now is . . . day of salvation* 2 Corinthians 6:2 (KJV)

p. 81 *Like stretching palm-groves . . . abundant water* Numbers 24:6–7a (AUTHOR'S RENDERING)

p. 82 *Lightly as a falling star . . . bowl of golden fruit* From the poem "A Blessing for the New Baby," by Luci Shaw, in *Accompanied by Angels* (Grand Rapids, MI: Wm. B. Eerdmans, 2006), 22.

p. 82 *Whoever wishes to be great among you must be your servant.* Matthew 20:26 (NRSV)

p. 82 *Unless a grain of wheat . . . many times over* John 12:24 (THE MESSAGE)

p. 83 *soiled, defiled, oppressing* Zephaniah 3:1 (NRSV)

p. 83 *The LORD . . . with loud singing* Zephaniah 3:17 (NRSV)

p. 83 *At that time . . . with one accord* Zephaniah 3:9 (NRSV)

p. 83 *Therefore wait . . . as a witness* Zephaniah 3:8a (NRSV)

p. 84 *You did the unthinkable . . . link the unlinkable* From the poem "Step on It," by Luci Shaw, from *Polishing the Petoskey Stone* (Vancouver, BC: Regent College Publishing, 2003), 100.

p. 88 *Turn to me . . . there is no other* Isaiah 45:22 (NRSV)

p. 88 *Are you the one . . . wait for another?* Matthew 11:3 (NRSV)

p. 88 *Lord, to whom can we go? . . . eternal life* John 6:68 (NRSV)

p. 89 *The least . . . is greater than he* Luke 7:28 (NRSV)

p. 89 *the Beatitudes* Luke 6:20–23 (NRSV)

p. 90 *Enlarge . . . and to the left* Adapted from Isaiah 54:2–3 (NRSV)

p. 90 *his Father's business* See Luke 2:49 (KJV)

Fourth Week of Advent

p. 102 *Look, the young woman . . . name him Immanuel* Isaiah 7:14 (NRSV)

p. 102 *. . . called to . . . be saints* See Romans 1:6–7 (NRSV)

p. 106 *The days are surely coming . . . righteousness in his wake* See Jeremiah 33:14–15 (NRSV)

p. 107 Denise Levertov, from *A Door in the Hive*, (New York: New Directions, 1997), 162–63. Reprinted by permission of New Directions Publishing Corp. Copyright © 1989 by Denise Levertov.

p. 112 *For now the winter . . . flowers appear on the earth* Song of Solomon 2:11–12 (NRSV)

p. 112 *Let me see . . . your face is lovely* Song of Solomon 2:14 (NRSV)

Notes

p. 113 *Blessed is she . . . by the Lord*   Luke 1:45 (NRSV)

p. 115 *The messenger . . . when he appears?*   Malachi 3:1–2 (NRSV)

p. 115 *the kings of the earth . . . able to stand?*   Revelation 6:15, 16–17 (NRSV)

p. 116 *And you, child . . . forgiveness of their sins*   Luke 1:76–77 (NRSV)

p. 122 *For my soul . . . near to Sheol*   Psalm 88:3 (NRSV)

Christmas through Epiphany

p. 137 *what we have heard . . . the Word of life*   1 John 1:1 (NRSV)

p. 145 *This man was . . . rested on him*   Simeon's story is told in Luke 2:25–35 (the quotations used here are from the NRSV).

p. 149 *desire of . . . the eyes*   1 John 2:16 (NRSV)

p. 149 *never left the temple . . . night and day*   Anna's story is told in Luke 2:36–38 (the quotations used here are from the NRSV).

p. 150 *those who do the will of God live forever*   1 John 2:17 (NRSV)

p. 151 *And the Word . . . grace and truth*   John 1:14 (NRSV)

p. 152 *From his fullness . . . grace upon grace*   John 1:16 (NRSV)

p. 155 *But Mary . . . in her heart*   Luke 2:19 (NRSV)

p. 157 *How good . . . collar of his robes*   Psalm 133:1–2 (NJB)

p. 158 *Even though our outer nature . . . day by day*   2 Corinthians 4:16b (NRSV)

p. 159 *See what love . . . God's children now*   The Scriptures in this reading are from 1 John 3:1, 2 (NRSV).

p. 161 *Rabbi, where are you staying?*   The Scriptures in this reading are from John 1:35–42 (NRSV).

p. 162 *Even before a word . . . hand upon me*   Psalm 139:4–5 (NRSV)

p. 164 *For this is the message . . . love one another*   1 John 3:11 (NRSV)

p. 167 *Nations shall come . . . praise of the LORD*   Isaiah 60:3, 6b (NRSV)

p. 168 *In former generations . . . through the gospel*   Ephesians 3:5, 6 (NRSV)

p. 168 *When beggars die . . . death of princes*   *Julius Caesar*, Act 2, Scene 2

p. 172 *God's chosen ones . . . must also forgive*   Colossians 3:12, 13 (NRSV)

acknowledgments

I owe gratitude beyond words to David Goa and Greg Wolfe: their efforts made this book possible.

David gave me hope that the idea for this book had value. His friendship and spiritual mentoring enriched my understanding of Christmas and the Incarnation. He not only shared with me his deep knowledge of history and spiritual theology, but also introduced me to the profound contribution of Orthodoxy to the Christian tradition. Through our many conversations on the subject David helped me better understand the importance of time, place, and liturgical occasion. He also patiently introduced me to the world of art. David spent hours identifying many of the images used to illustrate this volume.

Greg provided the tools that built this book. Without his network of relationships, editing abilities, knowledge of the publishing world, and passion for the subject, this book would not exist. He was tireless in his labors and gracious in dealing with the stumblings of a neophyte. In moments when despair seemed to be setting in, Greg's wisdom and practical perspective rekindled hope.

Many thanks also to the authors who so graciously contributed to this book. They were selected because of their insight into the meaning of the Incarnation and their ability to write about it. The diversity of their vocations (poets, spiritual writers, pastors, and cultural critics) as well as their Christian traditions (Protestant, Catholic, and Orthodox) have come together in a beautiful and moving fashion.

Finally, I am grateful to John and Marion, Don and Ronna, Pauline, Maggie, Ken and Ruth, David J., Ken and Anne, Brian and Ellen, Jessie, Iain, Geraldine, Floyd and Janice, and Bruce for their practical support in making this happen. Thanks to Dean and Shirley, Jacquie, David and Marnie, Dave P., Pieter, Tim and Gina, and my family—your friendship, the joys and pains you shared with me, and your aesthetic sensibilities all guided my efforts to bring this project to fruition.

—GREG PENNOYER

contributors

SCOTT CAIRNS is the author of six poetry collections, including his most recent, *Compass of Affection* from Paraclete Press. His spiritual memoir, *Short Trip to the Edge,* relates his journey to Mount Athos in Greece. Cairns is Professor of English at the University of Missouri, and a recent Guggenheim Fellow.

EMILIE GRIFFIN is the author of several books on spiritual life, including *Doors Into Prayer*, *Turning*, and *Wonderful and Dark Is This Road*. With Richard J. Foster, she compiled and edited *Spiritual Classics*, an anthology of devotional readings. Her first full-length play, *The Only Begotten Son*, won the First Playwrights Award from the Louisiana Council of Music and Performing Arts.

RICHARD JOHN NEUHAUS, a Catholic priest and former Lutheran pastor, is one of the leading voices on religion and culture in America. He is the founder and editor of the journal *First Things*, and his books include *The Catholic Moment*, *The Naked Public Square: Religion and Democracy in America*, and *Death on a Friday Afternoon*.

KATHLEEN NORRIS is an award-winning poet and bestselling nonfiction author. Her books include *Dakota: A Spiritual Geography*, *The Cloister Walk*, *Amazing Grace: A Vocabulary of Faith*, *The Virgin of Bennington*, and the poetry collection *Little Girls in Church*.

EUGENE PETERSON is a pastor, author, and professor emeritus of theology at Regent College. He is the author of the popular paraphrase of the Bible, *The Message*, and has written over thirty books on theology. His current project is a five-volume series on spiritual theology; two titles have appeared: *Christ Plays in Ten Thousand Places* and *Eat this Book: A Conversation in the Art of Spiritual Reading*.

LUCI SHAW is the author of ten volumes of poetry and several nonfiction books, and is the writer-in-residence at Regent College in Vancouver, BC. Her poetry has been widely anthologized and has appeared in several publications, including *Weavings, Image, Books & Culture, The Southern Review,* and *First Things*.

CONTRIBUTOR PHOTOS: Scott Cairns: *Staff Photo from University of Missouri* | Emilie Griffin: *Luci Shaw* | Richard John Neuhaus: *Richard Nowitz* | Kathleen Norris: *Gregory Yamamoto* | Eugene Peterson: *Kate French* | Luci Shaw: *Kurt Scherer*

editors

BETH BEVIS is program coordinator for Seattle Pacific University's MFA in Creative Writing, and the editor of *Image* journal's e-newsletter, *Image*Update. A nonfiction writer, she received her BA in English from Seattle Pacific University and plans to pursue graduate study in English Literature.

GREG PENNOYER is a consultant on strategic planning, fundraising, and project development. He is the co-founder of the Centre for Cultural Renewal (Ottawa, Canada) and has recently become the project director for *Incarnation: A Recovery of Meaning* (an international art exhibition).

GREGORY WOLFE is Writer in Residence at Seattle Pacific University and the founder and editor of *Image*, one of America's leading literary quarterlies. He also directs the Master of Fine Arts in Creative Writing at SPU. In 2005 he served as a judge for the National Book Awards. Among his books are *Intruding Upon the Timeless: Meditations on Art, Faith, and Mystery* and *Malcolm Muggeridge: A Biography*.

illustrations

List of Illustrations

about Paraclete Press

Who We Are

Paraclete Press is an ecumenical publisher of books and recordings on Christian spirituality. Our publishing represents a full expression of Christian belief and practice—from Catholic to Evangelical, from Protestant to Orthodox.

Paraclete Press is the publishing arm of the Community of Jesus, an ecumenical monastic community in the Benedictine tradition. As such, we are uniquely positioned in the marketplace without connection to a large corporation and with informal relationships to many branches and denominations of faith.

We like it best when people buy our books from booksellers, our partners in successfully reaching as wide an audience as possible.

What We Are Doing

Books Paraclete Press publishes books that show the richness and depth of what it means to be Christian. Although Benedictine spirituality is at the heart of all that we do, we publish books that reflect the Christian experience across many cultures, time periods, and houses of worship.

We publish books that nourish the vibrant life of the church and its people—books about spiritual practice, formation, history, ideas, and customs.

We have several different series of books within Paraclete Press, including the best-selling Living Library series of modernized classic texts; A Voice from the Monastery—giving voice to men and women monastics about what it means to live a spiritual life today; award-winning literary faith fiction; and books that explore Judaism and Islam and discover how these faiths inform Christian thought and practice.

Recordings From Gregorian chant to contemporary American choral works, our music recordings celebrate the richness of sacred choral music through the centuries. Paraclete is proud to distribute the recordings of the internationally acclaimed choir Gloriæ Dei Cantores, who have been praised for their "rapt and fathomless spiritual intensity" by *American Record Guide*, and the Gloriæ Dei Cantores Schola, which specializes in the study and performance of Gregorian chant. Paraclete is also the exclusive North American distributor of the recordings of the Monastic Choir of St. Peter's Abbey in Solesmes, France, long considered to be a leading authority on Gregorian chant performance.

Learn more about us at our Web site: www.paracletepress.com *or call us toll-free at* 1-800-451-5006.